A^{my}roma Rice COOKER COOKBOOK

135 Tried and True, Incredible Recipes

By

Amy Bradshaw

Table of Contents

1

AROMA RICE COOKER INTRODUCTION

Recipe Selections

This selection of rice cooker recipes for the Aroma rice cooker includes dishes from popular cuisines from around the world. The main recipe categories that are included in this selection are from Asia, Europe, the Middle East and the US. These unique versions of rice cooker recipes are easy to prepare and require less supervision while cooking your favorite dishes at home. Cooking food with a rice cooker is also safe and healthy. It is healthy in that the nutrients in the food are retained during the cooking process.

These delicious recipes also include famous rice, breakfast, lunch and dinner recipes from around the world. You can choose from Asian recipes which include a wide variety of mouth-watering and flavorful dishes from all over Asia. The selection also includes Middle Eastern recipes that are rich in flavor and very filling. And if you want to have some light meals but still with savory and decadent tastes, try the European recipes which can be prepared easily in a rice cooker but still taste gourmet. For savory foods that satisfy your appetite, this wide recipe selection also provides the best American dishes.

Benefits of Cooking with a Rice Cooker

The Rice cooker is of course used specifically to cook rice. But because of its unique features and convenience in cooking foods, more and more people use it to cook other dishes aside from rice. It has measuring cups for the right amounts of rice to use, and the corresponding water line located in the inner cooking pot for the required amount of water to ensure cooking success every time. And because it requires less supervision while cooking, it is convenient for busy people and allows them to work on other things at the same time. In addition to that, when the food is done it automatically switches to keep warm mode which makes cooking a worry-free task. It is also less likely to produce burnt food on the bottom of the inner pot and provides you with fluffy and perfectly cooked rice due to its accurate rice to water ratio.

But not only that, the rice cooker is also perfect for steaming and preparing soups, stews and chili recipes. The cooking process is the same as cooking rice but is more convenient, reliable and very safe. You can also use it to cook a complete course from side dishes, main dishes and even desserts. With a good rice cooker in your kitchen, you can also save money by buying rice in bulk.

Advantages of the Aroma Rice Cooker

With the unique features of the Aroma rice cooker, cooking your favorite rice recipes and dishes is easy and effortless due to the Aroma's programmable digital controls. It has also brown and white rice functions for you to prepare varieties of rice recipes.

And because of its' non-stick inner cooking pot, cleaning the appliance is very easy. It also has a delay timer feature which allows cooking dishes on the specific time when it is to be served. You can use this feature by setting the wanted number of hours for the food to be cooked and just leave it and come back when the dish is done. Cook rice or any other dish in the inner cooking pot and steam or reheat foods on the steam tray simultaneously.

2

How to Use the Aroma Rice Cooker

Basic Operations for Digital Controls

Delay Timer

The DELAY TIMER BUTTON is used for preparing dishes ahead of time according to the number of hours or the time wanted for it to be served. You can set the delay timer and come back when it is done and serve it right away, perfectly cooked.

White Rice Button

The WHITE RICE BUTTON is specifically used for all white rice varieties from short, medium, and long-grain types of rice that are perfectly cooked with restaurant-quality but prepared so easily.

Brown Rice Button

The BROWN RICE BUTTON is (you guessed it!) used for brown rice varieties which are very starchy which can make them tough-to-cook ordinarily. But with this unique feature and together with the delay timer, soaking brown rice is omitted by setting the delay timer with the equivalent amount of time for soaking brown rice ingredients.

Steam

The STEAM BUTTON is used for preparing steamed vegetable and other side dishes perfectly without worrying about overcooked foods because it automatically shuts off after the programmed steaming time has elapsed.

Keep-Warm

The KEEP-WARM BUTTON is used to maintain before serving dishes. And also very useful because it is automatically switched when the food is done which results in less burnt food on the bottom of the inner cooking pot and keeps the cooked food warm for up to 10 hours.

How to Cook Rice

1. Using the provided measuring cup, take the amount of rice needed and place it in a fine strainer.

2. Rinse with cool running water and drain thoroughly.

3. Transfer the rice into the inner cooking pot.

4. Fill the inner cooking pot with the corresponding amount of water using the line located on the inner pot.

5. Place the inner cooking pot into the rice cooker and stir to combine.

6. Close the lid securely.

7. Turn on the rice cooker by pressing the power button, and then press the white rice or brown rice button to start cooking.

8. The cooking indicator light of the rice cooker will illuminate and display a chasing pattern when the cooking process has started.

9. The digital display of the rice cooker will show a 12 minute final countdown before the rice is fully cooked.

10. When the rice is done, the rice cooker will produce a beep sound and automatically switches to keep warm mode. Remember to only limit for 10 hours in keeping the rice in keep warm mode.

11. Before serving, fluff the rice with the serving spatula and serve warm.

Water and Rice Ratio with Approximate Yield and Cooking Time

8-CUP AROMA RICE COOKER AND FOOD STEAMER RICE AND WATER MEASUREMENT TABLE

Uncooked Rice	Amount of Water in Pot	Approximate Yield	Cooking Duration
1 cup	Line 1	2 cups	White Rice: 26-35 min Brown Rice: 50-60 mins
2 cups	Line 2	4 cups	White Rice: 28-37 min Brown Rice: 65-75 mins
3 cups	Line 3	6 cups	White Rice: 30-39 min Brown Rice: 70-80 mins
4 cups	Line 4	8 cups	White Rice: 35-44 min Brown Rice: 75-85 mins

20-CUP AROMA RICE COOKER AND FOOD STEAMER RICE AND WATER MEASUREMENT TABLE

Uncooked Rice	Water Line Inside Pot	Approximate Yield	Cooking Time
2 cups	Line 2	4 cups	White Rice: 30-35 min Brown Rice: 100-105 mins
3 cups	Line 3	6 cups	White Rice: 32-37 min Brown Rice: 102-107 mins
4 cups	Line 4	8 cups	White Rice: 34-39 min Brown Rice: 110-115 mins
5 cups	Line 5	10 cups	White Rice: 38-43 min Brown Rice: 114-119 mins
6 cups	Line 6	12 cups	White Rice: 40-45 min Brown Rice: 114-119 mins
7 cups	Line 7	14 cups	White Rice: 40-45 min Brown Rice: 116-121 mins
8 cups	Line 8	16 cups	White Rice: 41-46 min Brown Rice: 118-123 mins
9 cups	Line 9	18 cups	White Rice: 44-49 min Brown Rice: 123-128 mins
10 cups	Line 10	20 cups	White Rice: 46-51 min Brown Rice: 125-130 mins

Note: All recipes listed are for the 8-cup rice cooker. When using the 20 cup cooker, simply adjust amounts and times according to this chart.

3

How to Use the Delay Timer

1. Each press of the delay timer is equivalent to one hour intervals. The delay timer of the rice cooker can be set from 1 up to 15 hours.

2. When the required time has been set, press the white or brown rice button depending on the variety of rice is used.

3. The digital display of the rice cooker will show a countdown of the expected time when the rice is cooked.

4. The cooking indicator light of the rice cooker will illuminate and display a cashing pattern when the cooking process has started.

5. The digital display of the rice cooker will show a 12 minute final countdown before the rice is fully cooked.

6. When the rice is done, the rice cooker will produce a beep sound and automatically switches to keep warm mode. Remember to only limit for 10 hours in keeping the rice in keep warm mode.

7. Before serving, fluff the rice with the serving spatula and serve warm.

How to Steam

1. Using the provided measuring cup, add the required amount of water according to the type of ingredient to steam in the inner cooking pot.

2. Locate the steam tray over the inner cooking pot and add the ingredient to steam on the tray.

3. Transfer the inner cooking pot into the rice cooker and close the lid securely.

4. Turn on the rice cooker by pressing the power button and then press the steam button. It will indicate 5 minutes initially and the next press will set 1 minute intervals. Set to the required steaming time to start cooking and after the time has been set the rice cooker will produce a beep sound to indicate that the steaming process has started.

5. When the water reaches a boil, the cooking indicator light of the rice cooker will illuminate and display a chasing pattern when the steaming process has started.

6. The digital display of the rice cooker will show 1 minute intervals from the time selected for steaming.

7. When the time selected has passed, the rice cooker will beep and automatically switches to keep warm mode.

8. To avoid over cooking, remove the steam tray carefully and transfer into a bowl with ice bath to stop further cooking.

Steaming Meat and Vegetable Chart

STEAMING MEAT

Meat	Water	Time and Temperature
Fish	2 cups	25 mins. / 140°C
Chicken	2 1/2 cups	30 mins. / 165°C
Pork	2 1/2 cups	30 mins. / 160°C
Beef	2 1/2 cups	Med 25 mins / Med-Well 30 mins / Well 33 mins. / 160°C

STEAMING VEGETABLE

Vegetable	Water	Time
Broccoli	1/2 cups	15 mins.
Eggplant	1 1/4 cups	30 mins.
Green Beans	1 cups	15 mins
Cabbage, Carrot, Cauliflower, Corn	1 cups	25 mins.
Peas, Spinach, Squash, Zucchini, Asparagus	3/4 cups	20 mins.

4

How to Cook Soups, Stews and Chili

1. Place all ingredients of the recipe into the inner cooking pot.

2. Transfer the inner cooking pot into the rice cooker.

3. Stir briefly and close the lid securely.

4. Plug the power cord into the electric source and turn on the rice cooker by pressing the power button to start cooking.

5. The cooking indicator light of the rice cooker will illuminate and will show a chasing pattern when the cooking process has started.

6. Use a wooden spoon with a long handle to stir the ingredients to avoid burning on the bottom of the inner cooking pot.

7. When the dish is done and cooking process is complete, switch to keep-warm mode to stop the cooking process and keep the food warm before serving.

Rice Cooker Tips

- When using the Aroma rice cooker for cooking, it is recommended to lightly spray or coat the inner cooking pot with oil for easier clean-up and less food stuck to the bottom.

- When the rice cooker has switched to keep warm mode and the rice or dish is not yet done, add more water if needed and reset the rice cooker to cook again. Manually switch to keep warm mode when the food is done.

- For added flavor and aroma, use equal amounts of stock or broth to substitute for the water.

- You can also add herbs and spices in cooking rice for extra aroma. Just place the herbs and spices in a spice sachet or wrap it in cheesecloth. Discard the spice sachet when the cooking process is finished.

- In steaming foods with the Aroma rice cooker, use extreme caution in lifting the lid to avoid steam burns and injuries from the high temperature of steam coming out from the rice cooker. Keep your hands and face away from the rice cooker in opening the lid.

- Also use a cloth in removing the inner cooking pot from the rice cooker after cooking.

- Use a thong and wooden spoon with a long handle in cooking dishes to avoid injuries and burns from the hot surface of the rice cooker.

- The provided serving spatula is only for serving and fluffing the rice, do not use this in stirring and sautéing ingredients.

- Do not place the inner cooking pot when wet into the rice cooker. It may damage the unit and may cause electrical problems and fire.

Rice Cooker Cleaning Tips

- Unplug the rice cooker after cooking and make sure that the unit is completely cool before washing.

- Remove the inner cooking pot, steam tray and other accessories from the rice cooker and wash it with warm water and soap.

- Only use a sponge or dishcloth in washing the accessories, wipe the washed accessories and all parts of the rice cooker with dry cloth.

- Remove the condensation collector and discard the liquid, and also remove the steam vent. Wipe with dry cloth and remember to reattach before using the rice cooker again.

5

RICE

Basic Rice Recipes

BASIC WHITE RICE

Recipe for 8 Cup Aroma Rice Cooker and Food Steamer

Cooking time: 28 to 37 minutes

Yields: 4 to 6 cups

INGREDIENTS:

2 cups of Basmati rice or any long-grain rice, rinsed and drained

Water, as needed to fill up to line 2

Salt, to taste (optional)

Fresh parsley, chopped for garnish (optional)

DIRECTIONS:

1. Using the provided measuring cup, take 2 cups of rice and place it in a fine strainer. Rinse with cool running water and drain thoroughly. Transfer rice into the inner cooking pot.

2. Fill the inner cooking pot with water up to line 2. Place the inner cooking pot into the rice cooker, swirl to combine and close the lid securely.

3. Press the power button to turn on the rice cooker, and then press the white rice button to start cooking.

4. When the rice is done, the rice cooker will produce a beep sound and automatically switches to keep warm mode. Let it sit for 10 minutes.

5. Fluff the rice and transfer into serving bowls or plates. Serve warm.

NOTE:

Do not exceed 10 hours in keep warm mode.

WHITE RICE PILAF, JASMINE RICE

Recipe for 8-cup Aroma Rice Cooker and Food Steamer

Cooking time: 28 to 37 minutes

Yields: 4 to 6 cups

INGREDIENTS:

2 cups Jasmine rice, rinsed and drained

chicken stock, as needed to fill up to line 2

¼ cup chopped almonds

½ cup button mushrooms, halved

1 shallot, minced

½ tablespoon butter or olive oil

1 garlic clove, minced

DIRECTIONS:

1. Using the provided measuring cup, take 2 cups of rice and place it in a fine strainer. Rinse with cool running water and drain thoroughly. Transfer rice into the inner cooking pot. Set aside.

2. In a pan over medium heat, melt in the butter and add the garlic and shallots. Cook for 2 minutes or until lightly brown and aromatic, and stir in the mushrooms. Cook for another 1 minute and remove from heat.

3. Stir in the sautéed ingredients and chopped almonds in the inner cooking pot with the rice. Fill the inner cooking pot with chicken stock up to line 2. Place the inner cooking pot into the rice cooker, swirl to combine and close the lid securely.

4. Press the power button to turn on the rice cooker, and then press the white rice button to start cooking.

5. When the rice is done, the rice cooker will produce a beep sound and automatically switches to keep warm mode. Let it sit for 10 minutes.

6. Fluff the rice and transfer into serving bowls or plates. Serve warm.

NOTE:

Do not exceed 10 hours in keep warm mode.

BASIC BROWN RICE

Recipe for 8-cup Aroma Rice Cooker and Food Steamer

Cooking time: 65 to 75 minutes

Yields: 4 to 6 cups

INGREDIENTS:

2 cups of brown rice (long, medium or short-grain rice), rinsed and drained

Water or chicken stock, as needed to fill up to line 2

Butter or oil, for greasing

Salt, to taste (optional)

DIRECTIONS:

1. Using the provided measuring cup, take 2 cups of brown rice and place it in a fine strainer. Rinse with cool running water and drain thoroughly. Transfer rice into the inner cooking pot. Season to taste with salt if preferred.

2. Fill the inner cooking pot with water up to line 2. Place the inner cooking pot into the rice cooker, swirl to combine and close the lid securely.

3. Set the delay timer for when the rice is needed to be served.

4. Press the power button to turn on the rice cooker, and then press the brown rice button to start cooking.

5. When the rice is done, the rice cooker will produce a beep sound and automatically switches to keep warm mode. Let it sit for 10 minutes.

6.   Fluff the rice and transfer into serving bowls or plates. Serve warm.

NOTE:

If your rice is too dry when the rice cooker switches to keep warm mode, adjust by adding water as needed depending on the texture of cooked rice. And cook further until it switches to keep warm mode, or until the rice is soft and moist.

If your rice is too moist or soggy when the rice cooker switches to keep warm mode, fluff the rice with the serving spatula and close the lid. Maintain keep warm mode for 10 to 30 minutes, or as needed until the rice is cooked through. Fluff rice occasionally to release excess moisture.
Do not exceed 10 hours in keep warm mode.

RED RICE

Recipe for 8-cup Aroma Rice Cooker and Food Steamer

Cooking time: 65 to 75 minutes

Yields: 4 to 6 cups

INGREDIENTS:

2 cups of red rice, rinsed and drained

Water or chicken stock, as needed to fill up to line 2

Butter or oil, for greasing

Salt, to taste (optional)

DIRECTIONS:

1. Lightly grease the inner cooking pot with oil or butter. Set aside.

2. Using the provided measuring cup, take 2 cups of wild rice and place it in a fine strainer. Rinse with cool running water and drain thoroughly. Transfer rice into the inner cooking pot. Season to taste with salt if preferred.

3. Fill the inner cooking pot with water up to line 2. Place the inner cooking pot into the rice cooker, swirl to combine and close the lid securely.

4. Set the delay timer for when the rice is needed to be served.

5. Press the power button to turn on the rice cooker, and then press the brown rice button to start cooking.

6. When the rice is done, the rice cooker will produce a beep sound and automatically switches to keep warm mode. Let it sit for 10 minutes.

7. Fluff the rice and transfer into serving bowls or plates. Serve warm.

NOTE:

If your rice is too dry when the rice cooker switches to keep warm mode, adjust by adding water as needed depending on the texture of cooked rice. And cook further until it switches to keep warm mode, or until the rice is soft and moist.

If your rice is too moist or soggy when the rice cooker switches to keep warm mode, fluff the rice with the serving spatula and close the lid. Maintain keep warm mode for 10 to 30 minutes, or as needed until the rice is cooked through. Fluff rice occasionally to release excess moisture.

Do not exceed 10 hours in keep warm mode.

WILD RICE

Recipe for 8-cup Aroma Rice Cooker and Food Steamer

Cooking time: 65 to 75 minutes

Yields: 4 to 6 cups

INGREDIENTS:

2 cups of wild rice, rinsed and drained

Water or chicken stock, as needed to fill up to line 2

Butter or oil, for greasing

Salt, to taste (optional)

DIRECTIONS:

1. Lightly grease the inner cooking pot with oil or butter. Set aside.

2. Using the provided measuring cup, take 2 cups of wild rice and place it in a fine strainer. Rinse with cool running water and drain thoroughly. Transfer rice into the inner cooking pot. Season to taste with salt if preferred.

3. Fill the inner cooking pot with water up to line 2. Place the inner cooking pot into the rice cooker, swirl to combine and close the lid securely.

4. Set the delay timer for when the rice is needed to be served.

5. Press the power button to turn on the rice cooker, and then press the brown rice button to start cooking.

6. When the rice is done, the rice cooker will produce a beep sound and automatically switches to keep warm mode. Let it stand for 10 minutes.

7. Fluff the rice and transfer into serving bowls or plates. Serve warm.

NOTE:

If your rice is too dry when the rice cooker switches to keep warm mode, adjust by adding water as needed depending on the texture of cooked rice. And cook further until it switches to keep warm mode, or until the rice is soft and moist.

If your rice is too moist or soggy when the rice cooker switches to keep warm mode, fluff the rice with the serving spatula and close the lid. Maintain keep warm mode for 10 to 30 minutes, or as needed until the rice is cooked through. Fluff rice occasionally to release excess moisture.

Do not exceed 10 hours in keep warm mode.

Asian Rice Recipes

CHINESE STYLE FRIED RICE

Recipe for 8 Cup Aroma Rice Cooker and Food Steamer

Cooking time: 45 minutes

Yields: 4 to 6 cups

INGREDIENTS:

2 medium onions, diced

1 garlic clove, minced

2 to 3 tablespoons olive oil

2 whole eggs, beaten

1 teaspoon light soy sauce

1 teaspoon fish sauce

½ tablespoon of sesame oil

1 cup cooked pork meat or chicken breast, deboned and cut into strips

1 medium carrot, peeled and diced

½ cup canned peas, drained

2 cups white rice, rinsed and drained

Chicken stock, as needed to fill up

2 spring onions, chopped

1 cup mung bean sprouts, rinsed and drained

Salt and pepper, to taste

DIRECTIONS:

1. Place the inner cooking pot in the rice cooker and turn on the rice cooker. Press the white rice button to begin cooking and add 1 tablespoon of oil. Once the oil is hot, add in the dice onions and

39

sauté until lightly brown and fragrant while stirring occasionally. Stir in the garlic and sauté for another minute, or until brown and fragrant. Remove from inner pot and set aside.

2. Whisk together the beaten eggs and light soy sauce, pour into the inner cooking pot and cook until lightly brown. Flip the egg and cook for another minute, or until lightly brown. Remove from inner pot, set aside to cool and chopped into dices.

3. Add 1 tablespoon of oil and add in the meat. Cook for 1 minute and stir in the sautéed onions and garlic, peas and carrots. Stir occasionally and cook for 2 minutes. Remove from the inner cooking pot and set aside. Return the inner cooking pot in the rice cooker and add in the drained rice.

4. Fill the inner cooking pot with stock up to line 2. Stir briefly, close the lid and press the white rice button to cook. When the rice is done and in keep warm mode, open lid and fluff the rice. Stir in the cooked ingredients, together with the sesame oil, spring onions and bean sprouts. Stir until well combined, stir in the eggs and season to taste with salt and pepper. Maintain keep warm mode for 10 minutes while stirring occasionally.

5. Transfer fried rice into serving bowls or plates and serve warm with extra spring onions on top if desired.

THAI FRIED RICE WITH PRAWNS AND PEAS

Recipe for 8 Cup Aroma Rice Cooker and Food Steamer

Cooking time: 40 to 45 minutes

Yields: 4 to 6 cups

INGREDIENTS:

2 tablespoons of oil

1 medium onion, halved and thinly sliced

2 garlic cloves, minced

1 red hot chili, chopped

1 cup raw prawns, peeled and deveined

2 cups brown rice, soaked and drained

Water, as needed to fill up to line 2

½ cup canned peas, drained

1 tablespoon light soy sauce

1 tablespoon fish sauce

½ cup loosely packed fresh coriander, chopped

4 large whole eggs, beaten

Hot chili sauce, as needed for extra heat (optional)

DIRECTIONS:

1. Drain the soaked brown rice a couple of hours before cooking the Thai Fried Rice. Place into the inner pot and fill with eater up to line 2. Place the inner pot in the rice cooker, turn on and press brown rice button to start cooking. Set delay timer for when the rice is needed to be served. Once the rice is ready, turn off cooker

and fluff with serving spatula. Transfer into a bowl or plate and set aside.

2. Wash the inner cooking pot and wipe with cloth. Place it into the rice cooker, turn on and press brown rice button to start cooking the fried rice recipe. Add a tablespoon of oil and add in the beaten egg, cook until lightly brown and flip to cook the other side for another minute. Remove from the inner pot, set aside to cool and chop into small pieces.

3. Add and heat in 1 tablespoon of oil, add in the onion, garlic and chili and sauté until soft and fragrant, for about 2 minutes. Add the prawns and cook until opaque in color, stir in the peas and rice. Season to taste with salt and pepper if desired, stir in ¾ of coriander and cook for about 3 minutes while stirring occasionally. Remove from the inner cooking pot.

4. Portion fried rice into individual serving bowls. Serve with the eggs, prawns, coriander on top and chili sauce if preferred.

Benihana Japanese Fried Rice

Recipe for 8 Cup Aroma Rice Cooker and Food Steamer

Cooking time: 40 to 45 minutes

Yields: 4 to 6 cups

INGREDIENTS:

2 cups of white long-grain rice, rinsed and drained

Water or chicken stock, as needed to fill up to line 2

1 cup canned peas, drained

1 small carrot, peeled and diced

2 whole eggs, lightly beaten

2 medium onions, diced

2 tablespoons of butter

2 tablespoons light soy sauce

Salt and pepper, to taste

DIRECTIONS:

1. Rinse and drain the rice and place into the inner cooking pot. Fill with water or stock up to line 2 and place inner pot in the rice cooker. Season to taste with salt and pepper, if desired. Turn on rice cooker and press the white rice button to start cooking. Once the rice is done, fluff with a serving spatula, transfer on large bowl and set aside.

2. Wash the inner cooking pot and wipe with cloth. Return in the rice cooker, turn on and press the white button to start cooking. Add and melt in 1 tablespoon of butter, fry the eggs while cooking and making the eggs into smaller pieces with a wooden

43

spoon or serving spatula. Remove from the inner pot and set aside.

3. Melt the remaining butter in the inner pot and stir in the onions, carrots and peas. Cook for 5 minutes while stirring regularly or until the peas and carrots and tender and cooked through.

4. Stir in the rice, eggs, lights soy sauce and season to taste with salt and pepper. Cook for another 2 minutes and stir the ingredients until well combined. Remove the inner cooking pot from the rice cooker.

5. Portion fried rice into individual serving bowls or plates and serve warm with extra soy sauce in a separate bowl.

LEBANESE LENTIL/RICE PILAF WITH BLACKENED ONIONS

Recipe for 8 Cup Aroma Rice Cooker and Food Steamer

Cooking time: 40 to 45 minutes

Yields: 4 to 6 cups

INGREDIENTS:

3 tablespoons of olive oil, divided

1 large purple onion, diced

2 garlic cloves, minced

½ tablespoon cumin powder

½ teaspoon cinnamon powder

½ teaspoon allspice mix

Vegetable broth or chicken stock, as needed to fill up to line 2

½ cup dried lentils, rinsed and drained

2 cups long-grain white rice

2 purple onions, halved and thinly sliced

3 ripe tomatoes, quartered and seeded

1 cucumber, peeled and sliced into thin rounds

Plain yogurt, for serving

Fresh mint leaves, for garnish

DIRECTIONS:

1. Rinse and drain the rice, place into a bowl set aside.

2. Place the inner cooking pot in the rice cooker, turn on and press the white rice button to start cooking. Add and heat in half of the oil, add the thinly sliced onions and cook until caramelized and starts to darken in color, for about 15 to 20 minutes. Remove from the inner cooking pot and set aside.

3. Wash and clean the inner cooking pot, and the wipe with cloth. Return the inner cooking pot into the rice cooker, turn on and press the white rice button to start cooking. Add half of the oil and sauté in the garlic, diced onions, cinnamon spice, allspice mix and cumin powder. Pour in 1 cup of broth or stock and add the lentils, close the lid and bring to a boil. Stir in the rice and add more broth or stock up to line 2, close lid and wait until the rice is cooked through. When the rice is done, season to taste with salt and pepper. Fluff with a serving spatula and maintain keep warm mode for 10 minutes.

4. Portion into individual serving plates, top with blackened onions and mint leaves. Serve warm with sliced tomatoes and cucumbers on the sides, and yogurt on top, or in a separate bowl.

GINGERED CHICKEN RICE

Recipe for 8 Cup Aroma Rice Cooker and Food Steamer

Cooking time: 40 to 45 minutes

Yields: 4 to 6 cups

INGREDIENTS:

1 tablespoon of ghee or oil

Hot water or chicken stock, as needed to fill up to line 2

2 cups of Jasmine rice, rinsed and drained

2 chicken thighs, skinned and deboned, cubed into 1-inch pieces

2 pieces of 1-inch fresh ginger root, peeled and cut into juliennes

2 cups tightly packed baby spinach, rinsed

1 cup of fresh coconut milk, or canned if unavailable

Salt and pepper, to taste

Fresh parsley leaves, chopped for garnish

DIRECTIONS:

1. Rinse and drain the rice, place into a bowl and set aside. Skin and debone chicken, cut into cubes and season with salt and pepper.

2. Place the inner cooking pot in the rice cooker, turn on and press the white rice button to start cooking. Add the ghee and fry the chicken until brown while stirring occasionally. Turn off the rice cooker and remove meat from the inner cooking pot, transfer into bowl and set aside.

3. Place the drained rice, ginger and chicken in the inner cooking pot and place it in the rice cooker. Pour in the coconut milk and fill with stock up to line 2. Place and arrange the baby spinach on

top, season to taste with salt and pepper and close the lid. Turn on the rice cooker and press the white rice button to start cooking.

4. When the rice is done, fluff with a serving spatula and check for doneness. If the rice is too moist, fluff and cook press the white rice button to cook further until it switches to keep warm mode. If the rice is too dry, add ½ cup of liquid and fluff the rice. Close the lid and maintain keep warm mode until the rice is soft. Let it rest for 10 minutes.

5. Portion into individual serving bowls, serve warm with chopped parsley on top.

Middle Eastern Rice Recipes

MIDDLE EASTERN RICE WITH BLACK BEANS AND CHICKPEAS

Recipe for 8 Cup Aroma Rice Cooker and Food Steamer

Cooking time: 40 to 45 minutes

Yields: 4 to 6 cups

INGREDIENTS:

1 tablespoon of ghee or oil

1 garlic clove, minced

2 cups Basmati rice, rinsed and drained

½ tablespoon cumin powder

½ tablespoon coriander powder

½ tablespoon turmeric powder

½ tablespoon cayenne pepper

Chicken stock, as needed to fill up to line 2

2 cups of ground turkey

2 cups canned chickpeas, drained

2 cups canned black beans, drained

1 cup loosely packed fresh cilantro, chopped (optional)

1 cup loosely packed fresh parsley leaves, chopped (optional)

¼ cup of toasted pine nuts (optional)

Salt and freshly ground black pepper, to taste

DIRECTIONS:

1. Rinse and drain the rice, place into the inner cooking pot and fill with stock up to line 2. Place the inner pot in the rice cooker, turn on and press the white rice button to start cooking. When the rice is done, fluff with a serving spatula and maintain keep warm mode for 10 minutes. Remove from the inner pot and place into a bowl, set aside.

2. Wash and clean the inner cooking pot and wipe with cloth. Return inner pot in the rise cooker, turn on and press the white rice button to start cooking. Add the ghee or oil, add and sauté the garlic until brown and aromatic. Stir in the cumin, cayenne, turmeric, coriander, ground turkey and season to taste with salt and pepper. Cook until the ground turkey is browned and most of the liquid has evaporated. Stir in the black beans, chickpeas, cilantro, parsley, pine nuts and the cooked rice. Pour in ½ cup of stock and briefly stir the ingredients, close lid and wait until the rice is cooked. Fluff rice with serving spatula, maintain keep warm mode for 10 minutes.

3. Portion into individual serving bowls or plates and serve warm with extra toasted pine nuts and parsley on top.

SAFFRON RICE

Recipe for 8 Cup Aroma Rice Cooker and Food Steamer

Cooking time: 40 to 45 minutes

Yields: 4 to 6 cups

INGREDIENTS:

¼ cup of toasted pine nuts

Water, as needed to fill up to line 2

4 to 6 saffron threads, soaked in 2 cups of warm water for 10 minutes

2 cups Basmati rice, rinsed and drained

½ cup seedless raisins

DIRECTIONS:

1. Rinse and drain rice, place in a bowl and set aside. Soak saffron threads in a bowl with warm water for 10 minutes.

2. Place the inner cooking pot in the rice cooker, turn on and press the white rice button to start cooking. Add the pine nuts and cook until lightly toasted and fragrant. Remove from the inner pot and transfer in a bowl, set aside.

3. Add rice in the inner cooking pot, pour in the saffron and soaking liquid. Add more water to fill the inner cooking pot up to line 2, if needed. When the rice is done, fluff with a serving spatula and maintain keep warm mode for 10 minutes.

4. Stir in the toasted pine nuts and raisins, fluff again and portion saffron rice into individual serving bowls or plates. Serve warm.

CHICKEN MACHBOOS

Recipe for 8 Cup Aroma Rice Cooker and Food Steamer

Cooking time: 40 to 45 minutes

Yields: 4 to 6 cups

INGREDIENTS:

2 medium purple onions, diced

2 tablespoons clarified butter or ghee

2 to 3 teaspoons Baharat spice mix

½ tablespoon ground turmeric

2 tablespoons oil

2 chicken thighs

2 chicken legs

1 jalapeno, seeded and diced

1-inch fresh ginger root, minced

5 garlic cloves, crushed and sliced

1 cup canned stewed tomatoes, drained

2 Loomi or dried limes, punctured

4 pods of green cardamom

½ teaspoon cloves, ground

1 cinnamon stick

1 tablespoon salt

3 cups of Chicken stock, or as needed to fill up to line 2

2 cups Basmati rice, rinsed and drained

½ cup loosely packed fresh cilantro, roughly chopped

¼ cup loosely packed fresh parsley, roughly chopped

Rosewater for sprinkling, for serving (optional)

DIRECTIONS:

1. Rinse and drain the rice and place it in a bowl, set aside. Season chicken with salt and pepper.

2. Place the inner cooking pot in the rice cooker, turn on and press the white rice button to start cooking. Place and arrange the chicken pieces in the inner pot and cook until brown and crispy, turn to brown and cook the other side of the chicken pieces. Remove the browned chicken from the inner pot with a thong, transfer on a plate and set aside.

3. Add the clarified butter in the inner cooking pot, add and cook the onions until brown. Stir in the garlic, ginger, jalapeno and sauté until soft and fragrant. Add the Baharat spice mix and ground turmeric, cook for 1 minute while stirring occasionally.

4. Bring the browned chicken in the inner cooking pot, together with the drained tomatoes, Loomi, ground cloves, cinnamon and cardamom pods. Stir in the parsley and cilantro and pour in the stock. Season to taste with salt and pepper and cook for 1 hour. Remove the chicken and transfer to a plate, set aside. Transfer the cooking liquid in a large bowl or pot, set aside.

5. Return the inner cooking pot in the rice cooker, add the drained rice and pour in the cooking liquid until it reaches to line 2. Close lid and cook until the rice is cooked through. Once the rice is done, check doneness and adjust texture by add more cooking liquid if the rice is too dry or cook further if the rice is moist. Portion rice on individual serving plate and top with chicken. Serve with a green salad and yogurt Raita, if desired.

DOLMADES (STUFFED GRAPE LEAVES)

Recipe for 8 Cup Aroma Rice Cooker and Food Steamer

Cooking time: 40 to 45 minutes

Yields: 4 to 6 cups

INGREDIENTS:

½ cup olive oil

1 large white onion, diced

1 fennel bulb, cored, halved and diced

1 teaspoon organic lemon zest

½ cup toasted pine nuts

2 cups long-grain white rice, rinsed and drained

Chicken stock, or as needed to fill up to line 2

¼ cup loosely packed fresh dill leaves, chopped

1/4 cup loosely packed fresh flat-leaf parsley, chopped

Salt and coarsely ground black pepper, to taste

1 cup of grape leaves, rinsed and drained

2 organic lemons, juiced

DIRECTIONS:

1. Prepare the stuffing mixture. Place the inner cooking pot in the rice cooker, turn on and press the white rice button to start cooking. Pour in half of the oil and add the onions, fennel and lemon zest and cook while stirring regularly until soft and fragrant. Stir in the pine nuts and drained rice, sauté for 2 minutes and stir ingredients to coat. Pour in the chicken stock

until it reaches line 2, close lid and wait until all of the liquid has been absorbed by the rice. Fluff the rice and stir in the chopped parsley and dill, season to taste with salt and pepper. Transfer to a large bowl and set aside.

2. Wash and clean the inner cooking pot and wipe with dry cloth. Return in the rice cooker, turn on and press the white rice button to start cooking. Add 2 cups of water or stock, close lid and bring to a boil. Place the grape leaves on the steam tray and place it over the boiling stock, steam grape leaves for 5 minutes or until pliable. Remove steam tray from the rice cooker, and switch to keep warm mode.

3. Pat dry grape leaves with paper towels and lay each leaf on a work surface, shiny-side down. Add 2 tablespoons of the rice stuffing, or depending in the size of leaf for easy rolling. Fold the edges toward the center and roll it upwards. You can also insert a toothpick to secure the stuffed grape rolls. Repeat the process with the remaining ingredients.

4. Place the Dolmades in the inner cooking pot, seam-side down and add in the remaining oil and lemon juice. Arrange and make an even first layer of Dolmades and then place a second layer on top, and so on. You may need to add more water to cover all of the Dolmades. Press the white rice button to start cooking, and cook until the rice are cooked through and tender.

5. Carefully remove the stuffed grape leaves and transfer into a serving platter. Serve warm.

MIDDLE EASTERN RICE (MEJADRA)

Recipe for 8 Cup Aroma Rice Cooker and Food Steamer

Cooking time: 40 to 45 minutes

Yields: 4 to 6 cups

INGREDIENTS:

2 tablespoons ghee or oil

½ tablespoons cumin seeds

1 tablespoon coriander seeds

2 cups Basmati rice, rinsed and drained (or any long grain variety)

Water or vegetable stock, as needed to fill up to line 2

1 cup canned lentils, drained

½ teaspoon turmeric powder

½ tablespoon cinnamon powder

½ tablespoon sugar

½ teaspoon salt, to taste

Black pepper, freshly ground to taste

½ cup fried shallots

DIRECTIONS:

1. Rinse and drain rice, place it in a bowl and set aside.

2. Place the inner cooking pot in the rice cooker, turn on and press the white rice button to start cooking. Add and heat in the ghee, add coriander and cumin seeds and cook until lightly toasted and fragrant. Stir in the drained rice and toss ingredients to coat rice with oil and spices.

3. Stir in the lentils and fill with water or vegetable stock up to line 2. Add the remaining ingredients except for the fried shallots, and season to taste with salt and pepper. Close lid and wait until the rice is cooked and switches to keep warm mode.

4. When the rice is done, fluff with a serving spatula and adjust seasoning if needed. Maintain keep warm mode for 10 minutes.

5. Toss in the fried shallots just before serving, portion into individual serving bowls or plates. Serve with extra fried shallots on top and yogurt.

European
Rice Recipes

ARROZ CON POLLO

Recipe for 8 Cup Aroma Rice Cooker and Food Steamer

Cooking time: 40 to 45 minutes

Yields: 4 to 6 cups

INGREDIENTS:

1 whole chicken, cut into 8 parts, skinned if preferred

Salt and ground black pepper, to taste

2 tablespoons of oil

2 to 3 tablespoons of tomato paste

1 green bell pepper, seeded and diced

1 onion, diced

3 garlic cloves, minced

2 red tomatoes, diced

Chicken stock, as needed to fill up to line 2

4 tablespoons of dry white wine

2 bay leaves

4 to 6 saffron threads, soaked in 1 cup warm water (optional)

2 cups of white rice, rinsed and drained

½ pound of asparagus spears, blanched and drained (optional)

½ cup canned peas, drained (optional)

1 cherry pepper or pimiento, seeded and diced (optional)

DIRECTIONS:

1.   Rinse and drain the rice and place in a bowl, set aside.

2. Season chicken pieces with salt and freshly ground black pepper, rubbing all areas with hands to evenly distribute the flavouring ingredients. Place the inner cooking pot in the rice cooker, turn on and press the white rice button to start cooking. Add the oil and brown the chicken on all sides; you may need to cook them by batch so as not to overcrowd the inner pot. Turn the chicken pieces to cook the other side, add in the tomato paste and stir to evenly coat the chicken. Remove chicken from the inner cooking pot, place in a bowl and set aside.

3. Add the onions, garlic and green pepper in the inner cooking pot and cook until soft and fragrant. Stir in the rice, diced tomatoes, bay leaves, wine, soaked saffron with liquid, 1 cup of stock and season to taste with salt and freshly ground black pepper to taste. Add more stock to fill the inner cooking pot up to line 2, place the chicken pieces in the inner cooking pot.

4. Close lid and wait until the rice is cooked through or switches to keep warm mode. Once the rice is done, remove chicken and place it on a plate and set aside. Fluff rice with a serving spatula and maintain keep warm mode for 10 minutes. Remove bay leaves and discard. Remove the inner cooking pot from the rice cooker.

5. Portion rice into individual serving bowls or serving tray and place the chicken on top. Serve with blanched asparagus, peas, and pimiento.

CHICKEN JAMBALAYA WITH CHORIZO

Recipe for 8 Cup Aroma Rice Cooker and Food Steamer

Cooking time: 40 to 45 minutes

Yields: 4 to 6 cups

INGREDIENTS:

1 to 2 tablespoons of oil

2 chicken breasts fillets, excess fat trimmed and cubed

1 red onion, diced

1 red bell pepper, seeded and sliced into strips

2 garlic cloves, minced

¼ cup cooked chorizo, chopped

1 tablespoon of Cajun seasoning

2 cups of long-grain white rice

2 cups of canned stewed tomatoes, drained

Chicken stock, as needed to fill up to line 2

DIRECTIONS:

1. Rinse and drain the rice and place in a bowl, set aside. Season chicken with salt and pepper, place in a bowl and set aside.

2. Place the inner cooking pot in the rice cooker, turn on and press the white rice button to start cooking. Add and heat the oil in the inner cooking pot and brown the chicken on all sides while stirring occasionally. Stir in the onions and cook for another 4 minutes or until the onions are soft and translucent. Add the minced garlic, tomatoes, chopped red pepper, chorizo and the Cajun seasoning. Cook for another 5 minutes, or until the

ingredients are soft and the chorizo is cooked through. Remove from the inner cooking pot, place into a bowl and set aside.

3. Return the inner cooking pot in the rice cooker, add the drained rice and fill with chicken stock up to line 2. Close lid and wait until the rice is cooked through and switches to keep warm mode.

4. Once the rice is done, stir in the half of chorizo mixture and half of the browned chicken. Fluff rice with a serving spatula and maintain keep warm for 10 minutes.

5. Portion rice into individual serving bowls, serve warm with reserved chicken and chorizo mixture on top.

Spinach, Mushroom, and Chicken Risotto

Recipe for 8 Cup Aroma Rice Cooker and Food Steamer

Cooking time: 40 to 45 minutes

Yields: 4 to 6 cups

INGREDIENTS:

1 tablespoon extra-virgin olive oil

Salt and coarsely ground black pepper, to taste

2 chicken breast fillets, skinned and cut into 1-inch cubes

2 cups tightly packed spinach, washed and drained

Chicken stock, as needed to fill up to line 2

¼ cup Parmesan cheese, grated

2 cups of Arborio rice or any starchy short-grain rice variety, rinsed and drained

2 cups of Crimini or fresh shiitake mushrooms, sautéed ahead

Salt and ground black pepper, to taste

DIRECTIONS:

1.   Rinse and drain rice and place in a bowl, set aside. Season chicken with salt and pepper, set aside.

2.   Place the inner cooking pot in the rice cooker, turn on and press the white rice button to start cooking. Add and heat the oil in the inner cooking pot, add the chicken and cook until lightly browned and cooked through. Remove from the inner cooking pot, place on a plate and set aside.

3.   Return the inner cooking pot in the rice cooker, add the rice and fill with chicken stock up to line. Add the spinach on top, close

the lid and wait until the rice is cooked through and switches to keep warm mode.

4. Once the rice is done, add in ¾ of the chicken, half of the grated cheese and mushrooms. Season to taste with salt and pepper, stir with serving spatula to combine and maintain keep warm mode for 10 minutes. Remove the inner cooking pot from the rice cooker.

5. Portion rice into individual serving bowls, serve warm with extra grated Parmesan and chicken pieces on top.

GREEK LEMON RICE

Recipe for 8 Cup Aroma Rice Cooker and Food Steamer

Cooking time: 40 to 45 minutes

Yields: 4 to 6 cups

INGREDIENTS:

2 cups of long-grain rice variety (Basmati or Jasmine rice), rinsed and drained

Chicken or vegetable stock, as needed to fill up to line 2

1 lemon, juiced

2 sprigs of fresh rosemary leaves

Salt and coarsely ground black pepper, to taste

Parsley leaves, chopped for garnish

DIRECTIONS:

1. Rinse and drain the rice, place in the inner cooking pot together with the stock, fresh lemon juice and sprigs of rosemary. Place the inner cooking pot in the rice cooker and close the lid, turn on and press the white rice button to start cooking.

2. Wait until the rice is cooked through and switches to keep warm mode. Fluff with a serving spatula, season to taste with salt and coarsely ground black pepper. Remove the rosemary and discard, close the lid and maintain keep warm mode for 10 minutes. Remove the inner cooking pot from the rice cooker.

3. Portion rice into individual serving bowls, serve warm with chopped parsley on top.

MEDITERRANEAN BROWN RICE RECIPE

Recipe for 8 Cup Aroma Rice Cooker and Food Steamer

Cooking time: 75 to 80 minutes

Yields: 4 to 6 cups

INGREDIENTS:

2 cups brown rice, soaked and drained

Water or vegetable stock, as needed to fill up to line 2

1 medium bell pepper (red), seeded and sliced into strips

1 cup of canned green peas, drained

½ cup raisins

1 sweet onion, diced

¼ cup of green olives, sliced or halved

¼ cup of vegetable oil

¼ cup of balsamic vinegar

1 tablespoon of Dijon mustard

salt and coarsely ground black pepper, to taste

½ cup goat's or Feta cheese, crumbled

DIRECTIONS:

1. Drain the soaked rice and transfer into the inner cooking pot, fill with water or stock up to line 2. Place the inner cooking pot in the rice cooker, turn on and set the delay timer to the time when the rice is to be served. Press the white rice button to cook.

2. When the rice is done, fluff with a serving spatula and maintain keep warm mode for 10 minutes.

3. In a mixing bowl, mix together the strips of bell pepper, the peas, onions, green olives and raisins. In a separate mixing bowl, whisk together the mustard, vinegar and oil until smooth and thick.

4. Add and mix the balsamic dressing and vegetable mixture in the pot with the cooked brown rice. Season with salt and black pepper and stir to combine.

5. Portion into individual serving bowls or plates, serve warm with vegetables with crumbled cheese on top.

American Rice Recipes

WILD RICE WITH MUSHROOMS

Recipe for 8 Cup Aroma Rice Cooker and Food Steamer

Cooking time: 75 to 80 minutes

Yields: 4 to 6 cups

INGREDIENTS:

1 cup long-grain rice, rinsed and drained

1 cup wild rice, rinsed and drained

¼ cup of butter

Chicken or vegetable stock, as needed to fill up to line 2

1 large white onion, diced

1 cup of fresh mushrooms, trimmed and sliced or quartered

½ cup Marsala wine or dry sherry

1/2 cup loosely packed fresh flat-leaf parsley, coarsely chopped

Salt, to taste

DIRECTIONS:

1. Rinse and drain the long-grain and wild rice, place into a bowl and set aside.

2. Place the inner cooking pot in the rice cooker, turn on and press the brown rice button. Add and melt in the butter, sauté the onions until lightly brown and soft. Stir in the mushrooms and season with salt to taste, sauté until the mushrooms are cooked through and tender. Pour in the wine or dry sherry and cook until the liquid has been absorbed and evaporated. Remove from the inner pot, transfer into a bowl and set aside.

3. Place the mixed rice in the inner cooking pot and fill with stock up to line 2. Turn on rice cooker and press the brown rice button to start cooking. Cook and wait until the rice is done and cooked through, stir in the onion-mushroom mixture. Fluff with a serving spatula to combine and maintain keep warm mode for 10 minutes.

4. Portion into individual serving bowls or plates, serve warm with chopped parsley on top.

MEXICAN RICE

Recipe for 8 Cup Aroma Rice Cooker and Food Steamer

Cooking time: 40 to 45 minutes

Yields: 4 to 6 cups

INGREDIENTS:

2 cups long-grain white rice, rinsed and drained

Chicken stock, as needed to fill up to line 2

1 tablespoon of oil

1 white onion, diced

3 garlic cloves, minced

3 to 4 tablespoons of tomato paste

1 organic lime, juiced

½ cup loosely packed fresh cilantro, coarsely chopped

½ tablespoon of cumin powder

Salt, to taste

DIRECTIONS:

1. Rinse and drain the rice, place in a bowl and set aside.

2. Place the inner cooking pot in the rice cooker, turn on and press the white rice button to start cooking. Add and heat in the oil, add the diced onions and sauté until lightly brown and translucent. Stir in the minced garlic and cook until fragrant while stirring occasionally. Stir in the cumin powder and tomato paste and cook for 2 minutes more, stirring regularly. Remove from the inner cooking pot, place into a bowl and set aside.

3. Return the inner cooking pot in the rice cooker and fill with chicken stock up to line 2. Turn on and press the white rice button to start cooking. Close lid and wait until the rice is cooked and ready. Once the rice is done, stir in the tomato paste mixture, lime juice and ¾ of the chopped cilantro and then fluff with a serving spatula to combine. Season to taste with salt and maintain keep warm mode for 10 minutes and remove the inner cooking pot from the rice cooker.

4. Portion into individual serving bowls, serve warm with chopped cilantro on top.

DOMINICAN-STYLE YELLOW RICE

Recipe for 8 Cup Aroma Rice Cooker and Food Steamer

Cooking time: 40 to 45 minutes

Yields: 4 to 6 cups

INGREDIENTS:

1 tablespoon of oil

1 red onion, diced

1 green bell pepper, seeded and sliced into strips

2 celery ribs, roughly chopped

2 medium scallions, bias cuts

2 to 3 garlic cloves, minced

1 bay leaf

½ tablespoon of cumin seeds

½ tablespoon of ground turmeric

½ teaspoon of cayenne pepper

2 cups of long-grain rice, rinsed and drained

Chicken stock, as needed to fill up to line 2

Salt, to taste

¼ cup loosely packed fresh cilantro, chopped

½ cup loosely packed fresh flat leaf parsley, chopped

DIRECTIONS:

1.   Rinse and drain the rice, place in a bow and set aside.

2. Place the inner cooking pot in the rice cooker, turn on and press the white rice button to start cooking. Add and heat in the oil, add the diced onions, green pepper, scallions and chopped celery and cook until soft while stirring occasionally. Stir in the minced garlic, cumin, turmeric powder, cayenne pepper and the bay leaf and cook until the ingredients are evenly mixed.

3. Stir in the drained rice, fill in with chicken stock up to line 2 and then season with salt to taste. Briefly stir to combine the ingredients and close lid. Cook and wait until the rice is cooked through. Once the rice is done, fluff with a serving spatula and maintain keep warm mode for 10 minutes. Remove inner cooking pot from the rice cooker.

4. Portion rice into individual serving bowls, serve warm with chopped cilantro and parsley on top.

SULLIVAN'S ISLAND BACON AND SHRIMP BOG

Recipe for 8 Cup Aroma Rice Cooker and Food Steamer

Cooking time: 40 to 45 minutes

Yields: 4 to 6 cups

INGREDIENTS:

1 cup diced smoked bacon

2 red onions, diced

2 cups of long-grain rice, rinsed and drained

Chicken stock, as needed to fill up to line 2

2 ripe red tomatoes, prepared into concasse

1 organic lemon, juiced

1 to 2 tablespoons of Worcestershire sauce

½ teaspoon salt, to taste

A pinch of black pepper, coarsely ground

A pinch of cayenne pepper

A pinch of ground nutmeg

2 to 3 cups of fresh shrimps, peeled and deveined

¼ cup loosely packed fresh parsley leaves, minced

DIRECTIONS:

1. Rinse and drain the rice, place in a bowl and set aside.

2. Place the inner pot in the rice cooker, turn on and press the white rice button to start cooking. Add the bacon and cook until crispy. Remove from inner pot and transfer in a plate lined with

paper towels to drain excess oil, leaving the cooking fat. Set aside to cool and chop into dices.

3. Add the onions and cook until soft and translucent, add the drained rice and stir thoroughly to coat evenly with oil. Fill the inner pot with stock up to line 2 and stir in the diced tomatoes, juice of lemon, cayenne, ground nutmeg, Worcestershire sauce and season to taste with salt and pepper. Return ¾ of bacon in the inner cooking pot together with the shrimp, briefly stir the ingredients to combine and close the lid. Wait until the rice is cooked through.

4. Once the rice is done, fluff with a serving spatula and maintain keep warm mode for 10 minutes.

5. Portion into individual serving bowls, serve warm with chopped parsley, shrimp and bacon on top.

DIRTY RICE

Recipe for 8 Cup Aroma Rice Cooker and Food Steamer

Cooking time: 40 to 45 minutes

Yields: 4 to 6 cups

INGREDIENTS:

4 links of spicy pork sausage, casings removed and chopped

1 red onion, diced

2 medium celery stalks, chopped

4 garlic cloves, minced

1 medium green bell pepper, seeded and diced

2 cups long-grain white rice, rinsed and drained

¼ teaspoon black pepper, coarsely ground to taste

1 tablespoon of Tabasco sauce or hot chili sauce

½ tablespoon of Cajun Seasoning, as needed for extra heat

Salt, to taste

Beef stock, as need to fill up to line 2

2 green onions, roughly chopped

DIRECTIONS:

1. Rinse and drain the rice, place in a bowl and set aside.

2. Place the inner cooking pot in the rice cooker, turn on and press the white rice button to start cooking. Add the sausage and cook until it starts to brown, stir in the garlic, diced onions, chopped celery and bell pepper and cook until the vegetables are tender and the sausage is cooked through.

3. Add the Cajun seasoning, Tabasco or hot chili sauce and coarsely ground black pepper and stir well to combine. Remove from the inner pot, transfer into a large bowl and set aside.

4. Place the rice in the inner cooking pot and fill with beef stock up to line 2. Return the cooked ingredients, stir to combine and close the lid, wait until the rice is fully cooked.

5. Once the rice is done, fluff with a serving spatula and maintain keep warm mode for 10 minutes. Season to taste with extra salt and Tabasco sauce, if desired.

6. Portion into individual serving bowls, serve warm with chopped green onions and extra sausage on top.

6

BREAKFAST RECIPES

Popular
Breakfast Recipes

GIANT PANCAKE

Preparation time: 5 minutes

Cooking time: 45 minutes

Yields: 4

INGREDIENTS:

1 cup of flour, sifted

2 tablespoons cup white sugar

1 teaspoon baking powder

½ teaspoon baking soda

½ teaspoon salt

1 large whole egg

¾ cup fresh milk

2 tablespoons butter, unsalted melted

Maple syrup, for serving (optional)

Fresh fruit, for serving (optional)

DIRECTIONS:

1. Mix together the sifted flour, salt, sugar, baking powder and baking soda in a mixing bowl. Set aside.

2. In a separate mixing bowl, whisk together the milk, egg and melted butter until smooth. Add the wet mixture into the bowl with the dry mixture, mix to combine.

3. Lightly brush the inner cooking pot with oil or butter and place into the rice cooker, turn on and press the white button to start cooking. When the oil is hot, pour the mixture into the inner

cooking pot. Close lid and cook for 45 minutes, or until browned and cooked through.

4. When the pancake is done, switch to keep warm mode and test doneness. When a toothpick inserted in the thickest part comes out clean, it is done.

5. Remove the inner cooking pot from the rice cooker and turn out pancake on a serving plate. Let it rest for 5 minutes before serving.

6. Slice the pancake and serve with maple syrup and fresh fruit on top, if desired.

SCRAMBLED EGG-TOMATOES WITH BACON

Preparation time: 5 minutes

Cooking time: 15 to 20 minutes

Yields: 2

INGREDIENTS:

2 medium whole eggs

1 tablespoon clarified butter

2 ripe red tomatoes, peeled and diced

2 tablespoons of crispy bacon bits (optional)

Salt and pepper, to taste

1 tablespoon green onion (optional)

2 tablespoons of grated Parmesan cheese (optional)

DIRECTIONS:

1. Place the inner cooking pot into the rice cooker, turn on and press the white button to start cooking. Add the clarified butter and stir in the bacon bits and diced ham. Cook for 1 to 2 minutes while stirring regularly. Stir in the diced tomatoes and cook further for 5 more minutes while stirring occasionally.

2. While cooking the meats and tomatoes, lightly beat the eggs in a bowl and add into the inner pot.

3. Briefly stir the eggs and meats, season to taste with salt and pepper and close the lid securely. Cook for 10 to 15 minutes or until the bottom part is lightly browned and the eggs are cooked through. Switch to keep warm mode and flip to cook the other side, if needed.

4.   Remove eggs from the inner cooking pot, transfer into a serving dish and serve warm with grated cheese on top.

RICE PUDDING

Preparation time: 10 minutes

Cooking time: 20 minutes

Yields: 4

INGREDIENTS:

2 1/2 cups skim milk

1 cups short-grain white rice, rinsed and drained

½ cup white sugar

A pinch of cinnamon powder

1 cup of skim milk, for serving

DIRECTIONS:

1. Rinse and drain the rice, place into the inner cooking pot together with milk, sugar and cinnamon. Place the inner cooking pot into the rice cooker, turn on and press the white rice button to start cooking. Close the lid securely and cook until the rice cooker switches to keep warm mode, or about 20 minutes.

2. Stir in 1 cup of milk and let it rest for 5 minutes before serving. Portion into individual serving bowls and serve warm with chocolate sauce on top, if preferred.

RICE COOKER HAM AND EGG

Preparation time: 5 minutes

Cooking time: 10 to 15 minutes

Yields: 4 to 6

INGREDIENTS:

8 medium whole eggs

½ cup heavy whipping cream

½ cup cooked ham, diced

1 green onion, roughly chopped

A pinch salt, to taste

A pinch of ground black pepper

1 to 2 tablespoons of melted butter

¼ cup of cream cheese

DIRECTIONS:

1. Whisk together the eggs and cream in a mixing bowl, stir in the ham and onions. Season to taste with salt and pepper and set aside.

2. Place the inner cooking pot I the rice cooker, turn on and press the white rice button to start cooking. Melt the butter in the pot and pour in the egg-cream mixture. Briefly stir the ingredients and cook until the mixture is set, or for about 10 to 15 minutes.

3. When the egg and cream mixture is ready, stir in the cream cheese and maintain keep warm mode for 5 minutes.

4. Remove from the inner pot and transfer into a serving plate or portion into individual serving plates. Serve warm with extra cheese and onions on top if desired.

5. In a large bowl, whisk eggs and cream; stir in the ham, onion, salt and pepper. In a large skillet, heat butter over medium heat. Add egg mixture; cook and stir until almost set. Stir in cream cheese. Cook and stir until completely set.

BREAKFAST OATMEAL

Preparation time: 5 minutes

Cooking time: 25 minutes

Yields: 3 to 4

INGREDIENTS:

1 cup rolled oats

1 ½ cups of milk, or as needed

½ teaspoon almond extract

1 teaspoon cinnamon

1 pinch salt

¼ cup maple syrup, divided

½ cup dates, chopped for serving

DIRECTIONS:

1. Add and mix all ingredients in the inner cooking pot, place the inner cooking pot into the rice cooker. Turn on and press the white rice button to start cooking.

2. Cook until the rice cooker switches to keep warm mode, or until the oats has absorbed most of the liquid. Adjust consistency by adding more milk if the porridge is too thick. Maintain keep warm mode for 5 minutes before serving.

3. Remove from the inner cooking pot and portion into individual serving bowls. Serve warm with extra maple syrup and chopped dates on top.

4. Place all ingredients, except dates, in cooker; stir gently to combine; sprinkle dates on top.

Asian Breakfast Recipes

KOREAN-STYLE SCALLION PANCAKES

Preparation time: 10 minutes

Cooking time: 10 to 15 minutes

Yields: 2 to 4

INGREDIENTS:

10 stems of scallions, cut into long pieces

½ cup flour, sifted

Water, as needed

½ teaspoon soybean paste

½ teaspoon sugar

2 to 3 tablespoons vegetable oil

DIRECTIONS:

1. Mix the flour and sugar in bowl, and mix in the water and soybean paste. Mix the ingredients thoroughly until well combined.

2. Place the inner cooking pot in the rice cooker, turn on and press the white rice button to start cooking and add the oil. Place and arrange the scallions in the pot to form a square or rectangle. Pour the batter on the bed of green onions. Cook the pancake until the bottom is browned and crispy while slightly pressing down with a spatula.

3. Turn to cook the other side and close the lid. Switch to keep warm mode, wait for 10 minutes and open lid. Remove from the inner cooking pot and transfer in to a serving plate. Let it rest for 5 minutes to cool, and slice the pancake into 2 or 4 equal portions.

4.   Serve warm with preferred sauce.

ASIAN BEEF CREPES

Preparation time: 15 minutes

Cooking time: 20 to 25 minutes

Yields: 10

INGREDIENTS:

2 ounces uncooked rice sticks (rice flour noodles)

1 teaspoon vegetable oil

1 tablespoon fresh lime juice

1/2 teaspoon chili paste or crushed red pepper

10 medium Boston lettuce leaves

10 Basic Crepes

1/2 cup shredded carrot

30 thinly cut slices seeded cucumber

30 mint leaves

30 cilantro sprigs

Marinade

1 1/2 tablespoons fish sauce

1 tablespoon minced peeled fresh ginger

2 teaspoons sugar

1 flank steak, sliced into thin strips

DIRECTIONS:

1. Combine together all ingredients for the marinade, transfer into resealable plastic and add the steak. Chill for at least 2 hours to allow the marinade mixture to penetrate in the meat. Remove beef from chiller, drain and set aside.

2. Place the rice sticks in a large bowl and cover with boiling water. Set aside and drain before use.

3. Place the inner cooking pot in the rice cooker, turn on and press the white rice button to start cooking. Add the beef and cook for 4 minutes while stirring regularly. Pour in the marinade and add the soaked rice sticks, lime juice and chili paste. Close the lid and cook for 10 minutes, switch to keep warm mode and set aside for 15 minutes to cook with low heat. Remove from heat and set aside.

4. Place the crepe on a work surface and place the lettuce leaf on the center. Top with beef and chopped vegetables and roll it up. Repeat procedure with the remaining ingredients.

5. Cut each roll into 3 equal portions, and serve with your favorite dipping sauce.

THAI MANGO WITH COCONUT STICKY RICE

Preparation time: 10 minutes

Cooking time: 55 to 60 minutes

Yields: 4

INGREDIENTS:

2 cups sticky rice, soaked and drained

1 ½ cup canned coconut milk

¼ cup white sugar, divided

½ teaspoon salt

½ cup coconut cream, for serving

2 ripe mangoes, pitted and sliced into short and thin slices

Toasted sesame seeds, for serving

Fresh mint leaves, for serving

DIRECTIONS:

1. In a mixing bowl, place the rice and add water to cover. Soak for an hour, rinse with running water and drain.

2. Slowly transfer the coconut milk in a glass bowl and let it stand for 5 minutes. When the thicker liquid or the cream has risen above the mixture, scoop it out and place it in a separate bowl. Set aside.

3. Place the soaked sticky rice in the inner cooking pot, add ½ cup of water, half the sugar and the thinner coconut mixture left in the glass bowl. Briefly stir the ingredients and place the inner cooking pot in the rice cooker, turn on and press the white rice

button to start cooking. Close the lid and cook for 20 minutes, or until the water has been completely absorbed by the rice.

4. When the rice has absorbed most of the liquid, pour in the reserved coconut cream into the inner cooking pot. Add the salt and stir the ingredients until well incorporated. Cook for another 10 minutes or until the liquid has been fully absorbed. Switch to keep warm mode and cook for another 10 minutes. Remove from the inner cooking pot and transfer into a bowl, cover and set aside.

5. While the rice is in the final cooking stage, prepare the coconut sauce for serving. Wash the inner cooking pot and wipe it with cloth, return into the rice cooker and press the white rice button to cook. Pour ½ cup coconut cream in the inner cooking pot and add the remaining sugar. Cook for 5 minutes while stirring regularly, or until the sugar has been completely dissolved. Remove the inner cooking pot, transfer into a bowl and set aside.

6. Portion the coconut sticky rice into individual serving plates or bowls. Add with mango slice and pour the creamy coconut sauce on each serving. Serve warm with toasted sesame seeds and fresh mint leaves on top.

BROWN RICE CONGEE WITH SHIITAKE MUSHROOMS

Preparation time: 10 minutes

Cooking time: 2 hours 20 minutes

Yields: 2 to 4

INGREDIENTS:

1 tablespoon cooking oil

2 garlic cloves, crushed and thinly sliced

1-inch fresh ginger root, peeled and julienned

1 cup fresh shiitake mushrooms, halved

1 cups long-grain brown rice, soaked, rinsed and drained

4 cups chicken or vegetable stock

1 head of Bok Choy, chopped

Soy sauce and chili paste, to taste

Ground black pepper, to taste

Scallions, chopped for serving

Roasted peanuts, for serving

DIRECTIONS:

1. Rinse and drain the soaked brown rice, place in a bowl and set aside.

2. Place the inner cooking pot in the rice cooker, turn on and press the white rice button to start cooking. Add and heat the oil, sauté the garlic and ginger for 5 minutes or until browned and fragrant while stirring occasionally. Stir in the mushrooms and cook for 2 minutes, or until soft.

3. Add the rice and stock in the inner cooking pot. Place the inner pot in the rice cooker and turn it on. Set the delay timer with 2 hours of more to soak and soften the brown rice, and then press the brown rice button to start cooking. Close lid securely and wait until the rice cooker switches to keep warm mode.

4. Check consistency of rice congee and season to taste with soy sauce, black pepper and chili paste, if preferred. If you want to have a thicker soup consistency, press the brown rice button and cook for another 10 minutes or until the desired consistency is achieved. Switch to keep warm mode and let it stand for 5 minutes. Remove the inner cooking pot from the rice cooker.

5. Portion the rice congee into individual serving bowls. Serve warm with chopped scallions and roasted peanuts on top.

SOUTHEAST ASIAN CRÊPES WITH CUMIN SEEDS

Preparation time: 10 minutes

Cooking time: 15 minutes

Yields: 4

INGREDIENTS:

1 cup all-purpose flour

¼ cup rice flour

¼ cup loosely packed curry leaves, chopped

¼ cup loosely packed fresh coriander leaves, chopped

½ tablespoon of cumin seeds, crushed

1 teaspoon salt

2 cups of water

2 tablespoons of butter

Whip cream, for serving

Fresh fruits, sliced

DIRECTIONS:

1.   Combine together the rice flour, all-purpose flour and salt in a mixing bowl. Mix in the chopped curry and coriander leaves and pour in the water. Continue mixing until well incorporated.

2.   Place the inner cooking pot in the rice cooker, turn on and press the white rice button to start cooking.

3.   Add and melt the 1 tablespoon of butter in the inner cooking pot. Once the butter has melted, slowly pour the batter mixture in the inner pot. Add with enough batter just to cover the bottom of the

pan. Cook the crepe until the bottom is lightly browned and turn to cook the other side for 2 minutes. Repeat the procedure with the remaining batter and the remaining butter if needed.

4. Place the crepes on individual serving plates. Serve with whip cream and fresh fruit slices on top.

Middle Eastern Breakfast Recipes

SHAKSHUKA

Preparation time: 10 minutes

Cooking time: 25 minutes

Yields: 2

INGREDIENTS:

½ tablespoon oil

2 garlic cloves, minced

1 medium onion, diced

1 medium zucchini, peeled and diced

1 cup canned crushed tomatoes

hot pepper sauce, as needed for added heat

4 medium eggs

a pinch of salt and ground black pepper, to taste

Fresh parsley, chopped for garnish

DIRECTIONS:

1. Place the inner cooking pot in the rice cooker, turn on and press the white rice button to start cooking. Add and heat the oil in the inner cooking pot. Add the onion and garlic, sauté until soft and fragrant. Stir in the zucchini, tomato sauce and the hot pepper sauce in the inner pot. Cook for 3 minutes or until the vegetables tender and the liquid has reduced, stirring occasionally.

2. Season to taste with salt and black pepper. Provide 4 spaces or make wells in the vegetable mixture, crack the eggs and carefully place it one at a time in the well. Close lid and switch to keep warm mode, cook until the whites are set and the yellows are still runny. Do not stir the mixture.

3.   When the eggs are ready and set, remove the inner cooking pot from the rice cooker. Let it stand for 5 minutes.

4.   Transfer the Shaksuka on a serving plate, serve warm with chopped parsley on top.

POTATOES WITH EGGS AND SPICED TOMATO SAUCE

Preparation time: 15 minutes

Cooking time: 45 minutes

Yields: 4

INGREDIENTS:

2 tablespoons oil

1 medium onion, diced

5 garlic cloves, minced

3 links of hot Italian sausage, casings removed and chopped

½ pound potatoes, peeled, halved lengthwise and thinly sliced

1 tablespoon Moroccan spice mixture (Ras el hanout)

Salt, to taste

2 cups canned crushed tomatoes

1 tablespoon hot chili pepper paste

4 eggs

Fresh Cilantro leaves, chopped for garnish (optional)

DIRECTIONS:

1. Place the inner cooking pot in the rice cooker, turn on and press the white rice button to start cooking. Add and heat the oil in the inner cooking pot, add the onions and sauté until tender and translucent. Stir in the garlic and sauté for 2 minutes until brown and fragrant.

2. Stir in the sausage and cook for 5 minutes, or until browned and cooked through. Mix in the potatoes and season to taste with salt

and Ras el hanout. Briefly stir the ingredient, close the lid and cook until the potatoes are soft and cooked through. Flip the potatoes occasionally to ensure even cooking. Stir in the crushed tomatoes and chili paste, cook for 5 minutes while stirring occasionally.

3.   Provide four spaces or make wells in the tomato-potato mixture, crack the eggs and carefully place it one at time into the well. Close the lid and switch to keep warm mode, let it cook for about 5 minutes, or until the whites are set and the yellows are still runny. Remove the inner cooking pot from the rice cooker.

4.   Transfer the potato and tomato mixture on a serving plate. Serve with chopped cilantro on top.

LEBANESE PITAS WITH MEAT STUFFING

Preparation time: 25 minutes

Cooking time: 20 minutes

Yields: 4

INGREDIENTS:

1 small white onion, finely minced

1 garlic clove, finely minced

¼ cup loosely packed fresh parsley, finely minced

½ pound lean beef, ground

1 ripe tomato, diced

A pinch of garam masala

¼ cup pine nuts, toasted

½ lemon, juiced

Salt, to taste

2 pita rounds, cut into quarters

1 ½ tablespoon olive oil, for greasing

DIRECTIONS:

1. Place the inner cooking pot in the rice cooker, turn on and press the white rice button to start cooking. Add and heat 1 tablespoon of oil in the pot, add and sauté the garlic and onion until soft and fragrant. Stir in the beef, garam masala and salt to taste. Cook for 5 to 7 minutes, or until the beef is browned and cooked through while stirring occasionally. Remove from the inner pot and place in a bowl, set aside to cool.

2.   Mix in the parsley, tomato, lemon juice, pine nuts, and parsley
       with the beef mixture. Stir to combine, set aside.

3.   Place 4 pita quarters on a work surface, add 2 tablespoons of
       beef mixture on each slice and cover with another slice of pita.

4.   Wipe the inner pot with cloth or paper towel and return into the
       rice cooker. Press the white rice button and heat in the
       remaining oil. Place the stuffed pita quarters in the pot, cover
       and cook for about 5 to 7 minutes, or until the bottom part is
       browned. Carefully flip the stuffed pitas and switch to keep
       warm mode. Maintain keep warm mode before serving.

5.   Remove the stuffed warm pitas from the inner cooking pot and
       transfer into a serving plate. Serve warm with Greek yogurt if
       preferred.

SPINACH AND FETA GOZLEME

Preparation time: 30 minutes

Cooking time: 10 minutes

Yields: 4

INGREDIENTS:

For the spinach

---

1 cup tightly packed fresh spinach

½ onion, diced

2 tablespoons olive oil

Salt and ground black pepper, to taste

¼ cup goats' cheese, crumbled

¼ cup Mozzarella cheese, shredded

For the dough

---

2 cups flour, sifted

1 cup of water

½ teaspoon salt

DIRECTIONS:

---

1. Combine the flour and salt in a mixing bowl, gradually pour in the water while mixing until the mixture comes together and doesn't stick to the side of the bowl. Transfer into a floured work surface and knead for about 5 minutes or until smooth and elastic. Roll out the dough and form into a ball, return into the bowl and cover with cloth. Let it rest for about 10 to 15 minutes.

107

2. While the dough is resting, place the inner cooking pot in the rice cooker, turn on and press white rice button to start cooking. Add and heat 1 tablespoon of oil in the inner pot, add in the onions and sauté until soft and fragrant. Stir in the spinach, season to taste with salt and ground pepper and cook until the spinach are wilted. Close lid and switch to keep warm mode.

3. Bring the dough into a floured work surface and divide it into 4 equal portions. Roll out each portion into thin rounds.

4. Portion the spinach mixture into 4 and add it on the center of the dough. Top with goat's and Mozzarella cheese and fold the dough into half, bringing the opposite sides. Repeat the procedure with the remaining ingredients.

5. Wipe the inner cooking pot with paper towels and return it into the rice cooker. Press the white rice button and add the remaining oil. Place the first 2 stuffed doughs in the inner pot and cook for about 7 minutes, or until browned. Flip it over to cook the other side for another 5 minutes. Remove from the inner cooking pot and cook the remaining stuffed dough. Return the gozlemes that has been cooked earlier in the inner pot and switch to keep warm mode. Maintain keep warm mode before serving.

6. Remove the gozlemes from the inner cooking pot, cut each into 2 portions. Transfer into a serving platter and serve with preferred dipping sauce.

MUSHROOM FRITTATA

Preparation time: 10 minutes

Cooking time: 35 minutes

Yields: 6

INGREDIENTS:

5 organic whole eggs

2 organic egg whites

¼ cup loosely packed fresh parsley, roughly chopped

½ teaspoon salt, divided

½ teaspoon black pepper, coarsely ground, divided

A pinch of nutmeg

½ tablespoon olive oil

3 red onions, diced

1 teaspoon of dried rosemary

2 cups mixed mushrooms, quartered

½ cup Parmesan cheese, grated

4 thin slices of Italian ham, diced

DIRECTIONS:

1. Place the inner cooking pot in the rice cooker, turn on and press the white rice button to start cooking. Add and heat the oil in the inner cooking pot, add the onions and sauté until soft and translucent. Season to taste with salt and pepper, and then stir in the rosemary and mushrooms. Close the lid and cook for another

8 to 10 minutes, or until the mushrooms are soft and cooked through.

2. While cooking the vegetables, whisk together the eggs and egg whites until well combined. Whisk in the parsley, nutmeg and season to taste with salt and pepper.

3. Pour the egg mixture over the vegetable mixture, cook for about 4 minutes and top with grated Parmesan cheese and diced ham. Close lid and switch to keep warm mode to continue cooking with low heat and to melt the cheese. Remove the frittata from the inner cooking pot just before serving.

4. To serve the mushroom frittata, remove it from the inner pot and cut into 6 equal slices. Transfer into a serving plate and serve with your preferred sauce.

European
Breakfast Recipes

LITHUANIAN PANCAKE RECIPE

Preparation time: 10 minutes

Cooking time: 55 to 60 minutes

Yields: 4 to 6

INGREDIENTS:

1 package of basic pancake mix

Additional ingredients for the pancake recipe

Whipped cream, for serving

½ tablespoon cooking oil, for greasing

Fresh strawberries and kiwi, sliced for serving

Honey, for serving

DIRECTIONS:

1. Prepare the pancake mixture according to package directions, set aside.

2. Place the inner cooking pot in the rice cooker, turn on and press the white rice button to start cooking. Wait until the inner cooking pot is very hot, and then add the oil.

3. Pour the batter mixture in the inner cooking pot. Close lid and cook for about 40 to 50 minutes, or until the top part is no longer wet. It is done when a toothpick inserted on the thickest part comes out clean. Switch to keep warm mode, and let it cook for 10 minutes more with low heat.

4. Remove the inner cooking pot from the rice cooker. Place a plate on top and turn it over to remove the pancake. Let it rest for 5 to 10 minutes before serving.

5.   Slice the pancake and top with fresh fruit slices. Drizzle with maple syrup on top and serve warm.

TORTILLA ESPANOLA

Preparation time: 10 minutes

Cooking time: 35 minutes

Yields: 6 to 8

INGREDIENTS:

½ cup oil, or as needed

4 medium potatoes, peeled and thinly sliced

1 white onion, minced

Salt and ground pepper, to taste

5 whole eggs

DIRECTIONS:

1. Place the inner cooking pot in the rice cooker, turn on and press the white rice button to start cooking. Wait until the inner cooking pot is very hot and then add the oil. Place the onions in the inner pot and sauté until soft and translucent, stir in the potatoes and cook for about 10 minutes while stirring occasionally. When the potatoes are tender and cooked through, season to taste with salt and pepper.

2. Add the eggs in a mixing bowl and whisk it briefly. Pour the egg mixture in the inner pot with the potatoes, and cook for 10 minutes. With a thong and spatula, carefully flip it over to cook the other side. Close the lid switch to keep warm mode, cook for about 10 to 15 minutes.

3.   Remove the inner cooking pot from the rice cooker and let it rest for 5 minutes before serving.

4.   Slice into 6 or 8 equal portions, serve warm.

CHORIZO HASH. BROWNS

Preparation time: 5 minutes

Cooking time: 15 minutes

Yields: 2 to 4

INGREDIENTS:

6 baby potatoes, skin on

3 strips of bacon, diced

1 link chorizo, sliced into thin rounds

1 cup of cherry tomatoes, halved

2 whole eggs

2 to 3 tablespoons of water

1 teaspoon oil

Salt and ground black pepper, to taste

1 avocado, pitted and sliced (optional)

Fresh parsley leaves, minced for garnish

Crusty bread, for serving

DIRECTIONS:

1. Place the inner cooking pot in the rice cooker and add the potatoes. Add water in the inner pot to cover the potatoes, turn on the rice cooker and press the white rice button to start cooking. Boil the potatoes until soft, remove from the inner cooking pot and rinse with cool running water to cool down. Cut the potatoes into half and set aside.

2. Discard the water from the inner pot and return into the rice cooker. Press the white rice button to start cooking, add ½

116

teaspoon of oil and bacon. Cook until the bacons are browned but still tender. Remove from the inner cooking pot, add the chorizo and cook until all sides are brown. Place the bacon and chorizo in a plate to cool, dice the bacons and slice the chorizo then set aside.

3. Place the boiled potatoes in the inner cooking pot, cut side down and flatten with potato masher. Cook until the bottom part is browned, and then flip to brown the other side. Season to taste with salt and pepper.

4. Return the bacon and chorizo with the tomatoes and gently toss to combine. Crack the eggs and stir it into the inner pot, add 2 tablespoons of water and close the lid. Cook for about 5 minutes, or until the egg whites are set and the yellow is still runny.

5. Adjust seasoning and switch to keep warm mode. Remove from the inner pot just before serving. Transfer into a serving plate, serve with avocado slices and parsley leaves on top.

SPANAKOPITA (GREEK SPINACH PIE)

Preparation time: 30 minutes

Cooking time: 1 hour

Yields: 5

INGREDIENTS:

2 tablespoons olive oil

1 medium onion, diced

¼ cup chopped green onions

2 garlic cloves, minced

2 cups tightly packed spinach, roughly chopped

½ cup loosely packed fresh parsley, chopped

2 whole eggs, beaten

½ cup goat's cheese

1 cup Feta cheese, crumbled

8 sheets phyllo dough

Olive oil, as needed for brushing dough

DIRECTIONS:

1. Place the inner cooking pot in the rice cooker, turn on and press the white rice button to start cooking. Add and heat the oil in the inner pot, sauté the garlic, onion, and green onions until soft and fragrant. Add parsley and spinach in the pot and cook for about 3 minutes, or until the spinach is wilted. Remove from the inner pot and set aside.

2. Combine together the goat's cheese, feta cheese and eggs in a mixing bowl and mix in the cooked spinach. Mix the ingredients and set aside.

3. Place one sheet of phyllo dough in the greased inner cooking pot, lightly brush with oil and cover with another sheet. Lightly brush the added phyllo dough and add with another sheet of dough. Lightly brush again with oil and add 1 more sheet.

4. Add the spinach mixture on the sheets of phyllo dough and spread evenly with a spatula. Repeat the process in adding sheets of phyllo dough on top of the spinach mixture.

5. Seal and join the edges with your fingers and place the inner cooking pot in the rice cooker. Close lid and cook for about 40 to 45 minutes, or until the bottom is browned. Switch to keep warm mode and remove from the inner cooking pot just before serving.

6. Remove the spinach pie from the inner pot, cut into wedges or squares then serve.

7. Preheat oven to 350 degrees F (175 degrees C). Lightly oil a 9x9 inch square baking pan.

ITALIAN-FRENCH TOAST

Preparation time: 15 minutes

Cooking time: 35 to 40 minutes

Yields: 4

INGREDIENTS:

For filling

1 tablespoons olive oil

1 garlic cloves, minced

1 cups tightly packed baby spinach

½ cup ricotta cheese

¼ cup Parmigiano-Reggiano cheese, grated

½ teaspoon of lemon zest, freshly grated

¼ cup loosely packed fresh basil leaves

¼ cup loosely packed fresh oregano leaves

Salt, to taste

Coarsely ground black pepper, to taste

For the toast

4 1-inch thick slices of French bread

2 medium whole eggs

½ cup whole milk

¼ teaspoon of salt

¼ teaspoon of garlic powder

1 tablespoon olive oil

1 cup of preferred marinara sauce, for serving

DIRECTIONS:

1. Place the inner cooking pot in the rice cooker, turn on and press the white rice button to start cooking. Add and heat the oil in the inner pot, add the garlic and sauté until brown and fragrant. Stir in the spinach and cook for about 4 to 5 minutes, or until the spinach is wilted while stirring occasionally. Remove from the inner cooking pot, place into a bowl and set aside to cool.

2. Mix in the grated Parmigiano-Reggiano and crumbled ricotta, zest of lemon, oregano and basil in with the spinach mixture while stirring the ingredients until well combined. Season to taste with salt and pepper. Set aside.

3. Make a shallow horizontal incision to form a pocket on each slice of bread. Carefully stuff each pocket with spinach-cheese mixture, and then gently press with your thumb and finger to close. Repeat the procedure with the remaining slices of breads.

4. In a shallow dish, add the milk, eggs, garlic powder and salt and whisk it thoroughly.

5. Whisk together the eggs, milk, salt and garlic powder in a shallow baking dish. Return the inner cooking pot in the rice cooker and press the white rice button to cook.

6. Add a tablespoon of oil in the inner cooking pot and wait until hot. Dip the bread slices in the egg mixture and coat evenly on all sides. Place 2 slices in the rice cooker and cook until golden brown. Turn to cook the other side and continue cooking with the remaining slices.

7. Return the cooked bread slice in the inner pot and switch to keep warm mode. Remove from the inner pot just before serving.

8.   Portion into individual serving plates, serve warm with marinara sauce on top or on the sides.

American Breakfast Recipes

MASHED POTATO PANCAKES

Preparation time: 20 minutes

Cooking time: 30 to 40 minutes

Yields: 4

INGREDIENTS:

1 cup mashed potatoes

2 small whole eggs, beaten in separate bowls

1 small onion, finely diced

Pinch of salt and black pepper, to taste

Flour, sifted for dredging

½ cup bread crumbs

2 tablespoons cooking oil, for frying

DIRECTIONS:

1. Combine together the mashed potatoes, one egg, onion and season to taste with salt and pepper. Mix the ingredients until well combined and divide into 8 equal portions.

2. Flatten each portion with both hands to form into patties. Dredge the patties in a bowl with flour, coat with egg and then with bread crumbs. Place it in a plate, set aside.

3. Place the inner cooking pot in the rice cooker, turn on and press the white rice button to start cooking. Add the oil and heat it until smoking, place the patties in the inner cooking pot and cook until the bottom part is nicely browned. Turn to cook the other side, close lid and switch to keep warm mode. Remove patties from the inner pot just before serving. You may need to cook the patties in separate batches to fit in the inner cooking pot.

4.   Remove the patties from the inner pot, transfer into as serving plate and serve warm.

CINNAMON APPLE OATMEAL

Preparation time: 5 minutes

Cooking time: 30 to 40 minutes

Yields: 3 to 4

INGREDIENTS:

1 cup steel cut oats

1 teaspoon cinnamon powder

pinch of salt

1 cup coconut milk

½ cup water, or as needed

½ teaspoon almond extract

2 to 3 tablespoons of local honey

1 apple, core removed and finely chopped

DIRECTIONS:

1. Add the oats, coconut milk, water, almond extract, 2 tablespoons of honey, cinnamon and salt in the inner cooking pot. Briefly stir to combine.

2. Place the inner cooking pot in the rice cooker, turn on and press the white rice button to start cooking. Close lid and cook until the oats have absorbed most of the liquids. Stir in the apple and add the remaining honey if needed. Adjust consistency according to preference by adding more water and cook until the desired consistency is achieved.

3. Switch to keep warm mode, let it stand for 10 minutes in the inner cooking pot to thicken.

4. Remove the inner cooking pot from the rice cooker. Portion oatmeal into individual serving bowls and serve warm.

PHILLY SCRAPPLE

Preparation time: 30 minutes

Cooking time: 60 minutes

Yields: 3 to 4

INGREDIENTS:

1 pound of lean pork, ground

1 cup cornmeal

1 tablespoon fresh basil leaves

1 tablespoon sage

½ tablespoon salt

¼ tablespoon garlic powder

¼ tablespoon marjoram

1 teaspoon black pepper

½ tablespoon nutmeg

¼ tablespoon onion powder

DIRECTIONS:

1. Place the ground pork in the inner cooking pot and add with water just to cover the meat. Place the inner cooking pot in the rice cooker, turn on and press the white rice button to start cooking. Boil the ground meat until it turns to grey in color and the liquid has reduced.

2. Pour the pot contents on a large bowl with a strainer on top. Place the meat on a separate bowl and set aside. Reserve about half of the cooking liquid and return into the inner cooking pot. Press the white rice button and bring the cooking liquid to a boil.

Gradually add in the cornmeal while stirring constantly to avoid lumps to form in the mixture. Return the ground meat in the inner cooking pot and cook for 30 minutes while stirring occasionally.

3. Stir in the seasonings and cook for another 2 minutes, or until well incorporated while stirring regularly. Remove the inner cooking pot from the rice cooker and let it rest to lower in temperature.

4. When the mixture has lowered in temperature, pour into a loaf pan and chill for at least 3 hours before serving.

5. Slice the chilled scrapple and fry before serving.

CAJUN-STYLE SHRIMP AND GRITS

Preparation time: 15 minutes

Cooking time: 1 hour to 1 hour 30 minutes

Yields: 6

INGREDIENTS:

2 cups regular grits

1 to 1 ½ cups chicken stock

3 cups water

3 to 4 links of Cajun Style Andouille, casings removed and diced

1 teaspoon salt

1 teaspoon black pepper, coarsely ground

2 cups of raw fresh shrimp, peeled and deveined

2 to 3 teaspoons Cajun seasoning

½ cup unsalted butter

1 cup white cheddar cheese, shredded

½ cup loosely packed fresh green onion, chopped

DIRECTIONS:

1. Place the grits, Cajun sausage, stock, water, salt and pepper in the inner cooking pot. Place inner pot in the rice cooker, turn on and press the white rice button to start cooking.

2. Season shrimp with the Cajun spice mix and mix it well with hands to evenly coat the shrimp. Place the coated shrimp on a steamer basket and place it on top of the inner cooking pot. Close

the lid cook for about 1 hour to 1 hour and 30 minutes, or until the shrimp and grits are cooked through.

3. Remove the steamer basket with the shrimp, transfer the shrimp in a large bowl and stir in the butter, green onions and the cheese. Melt the butter completely before serving.

4. Portion grits on individual serving plates or bowls. Serve warm with shrimp on top.

TEX-MEX MIGAS

Preparation time: 10 minutes

Cooking time: 25 to 30 minutes

Yields: 4 to 6

INGREDIENTS:

5 whole eggs

2 tablespoons butter

1 teaspoon milk

¼ cup jalapeno, chopped

1 small onion, diced

1 tomato, diced

1 garlic clove, crushed

4 corn tortilla

½ cup Monterey Jack cheese, shredded

Hot chili sauce, for serving

1 avocado, pitted and halved lengthwise, cut on the bias

Mango salsa, for serving

Salt, to taste

DIRECTIONS:

1. Place the inner cooking pot in the rice cooker, turn on and press the white rice button to start cooking. Melt the butter in the cooking pot then add the garlic and sauté with onions until soft and lightly brown. Stir in the tomatoes and jalapeno, close lid and cook until soft and cooked through.

2. Tear tortillas into small pieces add it in the inner cooking pot.

3. Whisk the eggs, 1 teaspoon milk and a pinch of salt in a mixing bowl. Pour it in the inner cooking pot, briefly mix to combine. Close the lid and cook for 2 minutes, or until the eggs are set. Switch to keep warm mode, stir and let it cook for 10 minutes with low heat.

4. Remove from the inner cooking pot and transfer into a serving plate. Serve warm with avocado slices and mango salsa.

7

VEGETABLE AND SIDE DISH RECIPES

Popular
Side Dish Recipes

WILTED SPINACH

Preparation time: 10 minutes

Cooking time: 30 minutes

Yields: 4 to 6

INGREDIENTS:

½ cup bacon, cooked and crumbled

2 medium onions, diced

2 tablespoons sugar

1 lemon, juiced

½ teaspoon salt

Freshly ground black pepper, to taste

4 cups loosely packed fresh spinach leaves, torn

DIRECTIONS:

1. Place the inner cooking pot in the rice cooker, turn on and press the white rice button to start cooking. Add the bacon in the inner cooking pot and cook until crisp and brown. Remove from the inner pot with a slotted spoon, transfer on a plate and set aside.

2. In the inner pot with bacon fat, add the onions, sugar, lemon juice, and then season to taste with salt and pepper. Stir the ingredients regularly and cook for 10 minutes, or until the onions are soft.

3. Stir in the spinach, close lid and cook for about 5 minutes or until the spinach is wilted. Open lid and stir in half of the crumbled bacon, switch to keep warm mode and cook for 5 minutes with low heat. Remove the inner cooking pot from the rice cooker.

4. Portion spinach on individual serving dishes, top with the remaining bacon and drizzle with extra lemon juice. Serve immediately.

STEAMED ARTICHOKES

Preparation time: 15 minutes

Cooking time: 30 minutes

Yields: 4

INGREDIENTS:

½ teaspoon of toasted fennel seeds

3 tablespoons of whipping cream

1 tablespoon Sherry vinegar

4 large globe artichokes, trimmed

½ cup loosely packed fresh parsley leaves

3 tablespoons drained capers, rinsed

2 shallots, chopped

2 garlic cloves, minced

2 tablespoons fresh tarragon leaves

1 anchovy fillet

½ teaspoon crushed red pepper flakes

½ cup olive oil

½ organic lemon, juiced

DIRECTIONS:

1. In a skillet over medium-high heat, toast the fennel seeds for about 2 minutes, or until aromatic. Remove from heat and transfer into a food processor, together with the capers, shallot, parsley, tarragon, pepper flakes and the anchovy. Pulse until a coarse mixture is achieved while scraping the sides regularly.

Transfer the mixture into a bowl and add the vinegar, oil and cream. Season with salt and pepper and whisk the ingredients thoroughly until well incorporated. Cover bowl and set aside.

2.   Rub the artichokes evenly with lemon juice on all sides and lightly squeeze to release the juice. Transfer into the inner cooking pot and pour in 2 cups of water. Place the inner cooking pot in the rice cooker, turn on and press the white rice button to start cooking. Cook for about 20 minutes or until the artichokes are tender and cooked through. Switch to keep warm mode, and cook for 10 minutes with low heat. Remove the inner cooking pot from the rice cooker.

3.   Place one artichoke on 4 serving dishes, portion the Salsa Verde into four serving bowls. Serve.

STEAMED BROCCOLI WITH BACON

Preparation time: 5 minutes

Cooking time: 15 minutes

Yields: 4

INGREDIENTS:

1 medium head of broccoli, detached florets

1 medium head of cauliflower, detached florets

salt and pepper, to taste

2 cups water, or as needed

1 tablespoon minced parsley, for serving

Crispy bacon bits, for serving

1 tablespoon lemon juice, for serving (optional)

DIRECTIONS:

1. Wash and drain the cauliflower and broccoli, cut into individual florets. Place vegetables on a steam tray and add 2 cups of water in the inner cooking pot, or as needed to cover. Place the inner cooking pot in the rice cooker and the steam tray on top over the inner cooking pot. Close the lid, turn on and press the white rice button to start cooking. Steam the vegetables for about 8 to 10 minutes, or until soft but still crisp. Switch to keep warm mode and cook further for 5 minutes with low heat.

2. Remove the steam tray with a mitt or cloth. Carefully remove the vegetables and transfer into a serving plate. Season to taste with salt and pepper and drizzle with lemon juice on top. Serve warm with crispy bacon bits on top.

COLLARD GREENS

Preparation time: 10 minutes

Cooking time: 1 hour

Yields: 4

INGREDIENTS:

1 tablespoon of extra virgin olive oil

4 slices of bacon, chopped

1 medium onion, diced

2 garlic cloves, minced

½ teaspoon salt or as needed, to taste

½ teaspoon black pepper, freshly ground

3 cups chicken stock

¼ teaspoon crushed red pepper flakes

2 stems spring onions, chopped

2 cups of tightly packed fresh collard greens, roughly chopped

DIRECTIONS:

1. Place the inner cooking pot in the rice cooker, turn on and press the white rice button to start cooking. When the inner pot is hot, add the bacon and cook until crisp. Remove with a slotted spoon and transfer into a plate. Let it rest to cool and finely chop.

2. Add the onions in the inner cooking pot and sauté until soft and translucent. Stir in the garlic and cook for 2 to 3 minutes, or until lightly brown and fragrant while stirring regularly. Stir in the collard greens and cook for 5 minutes, or until wilted while stirring occasionally.

3. Add the chicken stock and season to taste with salt, pepper and crushed pepper flakes. Cover lid and bring to a boil. Cook for 30 minutes and switch to keep warm mode. Maintain keep warm mode for 15 minutes to finish the cooking process with low heat. Remove the inner cooking pot from the rice cooker.

4. Portion greens into individual serving bowls and ladle in the soup. Serve warm with extra pepper flakes and spring onions on top.

BUTTER MUSHROOMS WITH BEER

Preparation time:

Cooking time:

Serves:

INGREDIENTS:

4 cups of canned button mushrooms, rinsed and drained

¼ cup of butter

1 cup of beer

2 tablespoons of fresh parsley leaves, chopped

1 teaspoon dried thyme

Salt and coarsely ground black pepper, to taste

DIRECTIONS:

1. Place the inner cooking pot in the rice cooker, turn on and press the white rice button to start cooking. Melt in the butter in the inner pot and add the button mushrooms. Gently toss to coat the mushrooms with butter and cook for 3 minutes.

2. Pour in the beer in the inner cooking pot, cover lid and bring to a boil. Cook for 10 minutes and then switch to keep warm mode. Stir in the thyme, 1 tablespoon of parsley and season to taste with salt and pepper. Close lid, stir occasionally and maintain keep warm mode for 20 minutes. Remove the inner cooking pot from the rice cooker.

3. Portion the mushrooms on individual serving plates, serve warm with extra parsley leaves on top.

Asian
Side Dish Recipes

STEAMED JAPANESE YAM CURRY WITH LIME

Preparation time: 10 minutes

Cooking time: 20 minutes

Yields: 4

INGREDIENTS:

4 to 6 small Japanese yams, quartered

1 tablespoon of fresh cilantro, chopped

1 tablespoon of lime juice

1 tablespoon toasted sesame oil

1 teaspoon of curry powder

¼ teaspoon salt, to taste

DIRECTIONS:

1.   Add 2 cups of water in the inner cooking pot and place it in the rice cooker. Turn on and press the white rice button to start cooking. Place the yams on the steam tray and place it over the inner cooking pot. Close lid and bring the water to a boil. Steam for about 15 to 20 minutes, or until the yams are fork tender.

2.   While steaming the yams, whisk together the lime juice, sesame oil and curry powder in a small bowl until well incorporated. Set

3.   Once the yams are done, transfer into a bowl and top with cilantro. Pour in the lime and oil mixture and gently toss to coat the yams evenly with the flavoring ingredients.

4.   Serve warm.

SAUTÉED WATERCRESS AND BOK CHOY

Preparation time: 5 minutes

Cooking time: 10 minutes

Serves:

INGREDIENTS:

1 tablespoon olive oil

2 to 3 garlic cloves, peeled and thinly sliced

½ pound watercress, chopped

1 cup loosely packed baby Bok Choy, trimmed and chopped

Salt and ground, to taste

¼ cup chicken stock or water

1 to 2 teaspoons of toasted sesame seeds

DIRECTIONS:

1. Place the inner cooking pot in the rice cooker, turn on and press the white rice button to start cooking. Add and heat the olive oil, sauté in the garlic for 1 minute while stirring regularly. Stir in the Bok Choy and watercress, season to taste with salt and pepper. Pour in the stock, cover lid and bring to a boil. Cook for 4 to 6 minutes or until the vegetables are wilted, switch to keep warm mode and stir in the toasted sesame seeds.

2. Transfer vegetables on a serving dish and serve warm with extra toasted sesame seeds on top.

CHILI SCALLOPS WITH BABY BOK CHOY

Preparation time: 5 minutes

Cooking time: 15 minutes

Yields: 3 to 4

INGREDIENTS:

1 ½ cups fresh sea scallops, rinsed and pat dried, thinly sliced

¼ cup chicken stock

1 tablespoon chili bean sauce

1 tablespoon light soy sauce

½ tablespoon cornstarch

2 tablespoons peanut oil

1 tablespoon of minced ginger

3 garlic cloves, minced

½ teaspoon salt

1 scallion, chopped

8 small heads of baby Bok Choy, base trimmed and chopped

1 medium red bell pepper, seeded and cut into strips

DIRECTIONS:

1. Combine together the stock, soy sauce, chili bean paste, and cornstarch in a bowl and set aside.

2. Place the inner cooking pot in the rice cooker, turn on and press the white rice button to start cooking. Add half the peanut oil, sauté the garlic and ginger for 1 minute, or until lightly brown and aromatic. Add the scallops and arrange them in an even

layer. Cook undisturbed for 1 minute, season to taste with salt and cook for another minute while stirring regularly.

3. Once the scallops are opaque but not yet fully cooked, remove and transfer on a plate. Set aside.

4. Add the remaining peanut oil in the inner cooking pot, and then add the bell pepper and Bok Choy then season with salt to taste. Cook for 2 minutes while tossing the ingredients, return the scallops and pour in the stock. Briefly stir and cover lid, bring to a boil. Switch to keep warm mode and wait for 10 minutes to cook further with low heat. Remove the inner cooking pot from the rice cooker.

5. Portion the scallops and Bok Choy on individual serving bowls, serve immediately with scallion on top.

PEPPERED SHRIMPS

Preparation time: 15 minutes

Cooking time: 15 minutes

Yields: 4

INGREDIENTS:

½ teaspoon of salt

2 cups fresh shrimp, rinsed and drained, peeled and deveined

½ teaspoon sugar

½ teaspoon Szechuan peppercorns, crushed

1 tablespoon peanut oil

3 garlic cloves, minced

1-inch fresh ginger root, minced

1 jalapeno chili, diced

DIRECTIONS:

1. Pat dry shrimps with paper towels. Set aside.

2. Combine together sugar, ½ teaspoon salt, and crushed Szechuan peppercorns in a mixing bowl. Set aside.

3. Place the inner cooking pot in the rice cooker, turn on and press the white rice button to start cooking. Add and heat the oil, sauté the garlic, ginger and jalapeno until fragrant. Add the shrimp and arrange them in an even layer, cook for 2 minute without stirring.

4. Switch to keep warm mode and stir in the salt mixture. Close lid and cook for 10 minutes with low heat. Open lid and briefly stir the ingredients. Remove the inner cooking pot from heat.

5. Transfer on a serving dish and serve immediately with extra crushed peppers on top.

STEAMED ASIAN DUMPLINGS

Preparation time: 30 minutes

Cooking time: 20 minutes

Yields: 8 to 10

INGREDIENTS:

20 to 30 wonton wrappers

Soy dipping sauce, for serving

Limes, halved for serving

1 cup water

For the stuffing

1 cup ground pork

2 scallions, chopped

¼ cup loosely packed fresh cilantro, chopped

2 tablespoons light soy sauce

2 garlic cloves, minced

1 tablespoon of rice vinegar

1-inch fresh ginger root, minced

1 teaspoon sesame oil

½ tablespoon sugar

½ head of cabbage leaves, thinly sliced

½ tablespoon black pepper, freshly ground

1 egg white

DIRECTIONS:

1. In a large mixing bowl, combine together all ingredients for the stuffing until well incorporated. Place one wrapper on your palm and add 1 tablespoon of pork mixture. Lightly wet the edges of the wrapper and with your fingers, join the wet edges to secure the stuffing. Repeat the procedure with the remaining ingredients.

2. Add 1 cup of water in the inner cooking pot and place into the rice cooker, turn on and press the white rice button to start cooking. Bring the water to a boil.

3. Place the dumplings on the greased steam tray and place it on the inner cooking pot. Close the lid and steam the dumplings for 15 to 20 minutes. Switch to keep warm mode and let the dumplings stay warm before serving.

4. Serve the steamed pork dumplings with soy dipping sauce and limes.

Middle Eastern Side Dish Recipes

FALAFEL CAKE CUCUMBER-YOGURT DRESSING OVER PITA

Preparation time: minutes

Cooking time: minutes

Serves:

INGREDIENTS:

2 tablespoons of olive oil

2 pita breads, cut into 2 portions

1 cup loosely packed fresh arugula

1 cup of cucumber-yogurt dressing

For the falafel

1 red onion, minced

2 tablespoons Dijon mustard

½ tablespoon cumin powder

½ tablespoon paprika

¼ teaspoon black pepper, freshly ground

¼ teaspoon salt

1 cup canned chickpeas, rinsed and drained

1 thick slice of whole wheat bread, torn into small pieces

1 whole egg

1 egg white

DIRECTIONS:

1. In a large food processor, combine together all ingredients for the toppings and pulse until a coarse texture of mixture is achieved. Transfer mixture on a bowl and set aside.

2. Place the inner cooking pot in the rice cooker, turn on and press the white rice button to start cooking. Add and heat the oil until smoking, pour in the chickpea mixture and close the lid. Cook for 10 minutes, or until the bottom is lightly brown and crispy. Turn the cake to cook the other side for another 10 minutes, close lid. Remove the inner cooking pot from the rice cooker. Place the cake on a plate, set aside to cool and divide into 4 slices.

3. Place the halved pitas on a work surface and put a bed of arugula on top. Place a slice of falafel over the arugula and spoon over with cucumber-yogurt on each slice of falafel. Serve immediately.

Syrian Green Beans with Olive Oil

Preparation time: 5 minutes

Cooking time: 25 minutes

Yields: 4

INGREDIENTS:

1 pound green beans

Black pepper, to taste

¼ cup olive oil

2 pita rounds, torn or sliced into pieces

¼ teaspoon salt, to taste

2 garlic clove, minced

¼ cup loosely packed fresh cilantro, chopped

DIRECTIONS:

1. Add the beans in the inner cooking pot, drizzle with olive oil and season to taste with salt and pepper. Place the inner cooking pot in the rice cooker, turn on and press the white rice button to start cooking. Stir the ingredients briefly, close the lid and cook for 15 to 20 minutes, or until tender and cooked through.

2. Open lid and stir in the garlic and cilantro. Cook for 2 minutes, or until the cilantro are wilted. Remove the inner cooking pot from the rice cooker.

3. Transfer the beans on a serving dish. Serve warm with pita slices.

OKRA MASALA

Preparation time: 20 minutes

Cooking time: 25 minutes

Yields: 3 to 4

INGREDIENTS

1 cup okra, base trimmed, rinsed and pat dried with paper towels, cut into 1-inch pieces

1 red onion, diced

2 ripe red tomatoes, diced

1 teaspoon of minced fresh ginger root and 3 garlic cloves paste mixture

1 teaspoon coriander powder

½ teaspoon of red hot chili powder

½ teaspoon of turmeric powder

½ teaspoon garam masala

½ teaspoon dry mango powder

Salt, as needed to taste

2 tablespoons of oil, for frying the okra

1 tablespoon oil, for the onion-tomato masala

1 teaspoon crushed dry fenugreek leaves crushed (optional)

DIRECTIONS:

1.   Place the inner cooking pot in the rice cooker, turn on and press the white rice button to start cooking. Add the 2 tablespoons of oil and heat until smoking, and add the okra and cook until soft

while stirring occasionally. Remove from the inner cooking pot, transfer on a plate and set aside.

2. Add 1 tablespoon of oil in the inner cooking pot and sauté the onions until soft and translucent. Stir in the garlic-ginger paste and sauté for 1 minute, or until aromatic. Add the diced tomatoes and cook until tender.

3. Stir in the dried spices one at a time and stir to combine. Close lid and cook for 10 minutes. Return the okra, crushed fenugreek, and salt in the inner cooking pot. Stir to coat the okra with the spice mixture, close lid and switch to keep warm mode. Maintain keep warm mode before serving the okra masala.

4. Transfer into individual serving bowls or dishes, serve warm with chopped cilantro and flat breads.

POLISH STUFFED CABBAGE RECIPE

Preparation time: 30 minutes

Cooking time: 1 hour 30 minutes on high, 3 hours 30 minutes on low

Yields: 6 to 8

INGREDIENTS:

1 large head of cabbage, leaves separated

1 cup cooked long -grain white rice

1 large whole egg, beaten

¼ cup fresh milk

2 medium onions, diced

2 cups ground lean beef meat

½ tablespoon salt

½ tablespoon black pepper, coarsely

1 cup canned tomato sauce

1 to 2 tablespoons brown sugar

1 lemon, juiced

1 tablespoon of Worcestershire sauce

DIRECTIONS:

1. Add 2 cups of water in the inner cooking pot, place inner pot into the rice cooker. Turn on and press the white rice button to start cooking. Bring water to a boil and blanch the cabbage leaves for 2 minutes. Remove from the inner cooking pot and transfer into a bowl with ice bath.

2. Combine together the rice, beaten egg, beef and onion in a mixing bowl. Season to taste with salt and pepper, and then mix to combine.

3. Place the cabbage leaves on a work surface. Add ¼ cup of beef mixture on the center, fold the sides and roll the leaves upward. Repeat the procedure with the remaining ingredients. Place the cabbage rolls on the inner cooking pot. You may arrange them in two layers to fit in the inner pot.

4. Whisk together the tomato sauce, lemon juice, sugar and the Worcestershire sauce in mixing bowl until the sugar is completely dissolved. Pour it in the inner cooking pot with the cabbage rolls. Close lid and cook for 20 minutes. Switch to keep warm mode and cook for another 3 hours with low heat.

5. Carefully transfer the cabbage rolls on a serving dish and serve with sauce on top.

CARROTS AND LENTILS

Preparation time: 10 minutes

Cooking time: 20 to 25 minutes

Yields: 3 to 4

INGREDIENTS:

3 garlic cloves, minced

1 cup lentils

1 large carrot, peeled and cut into sticks

¼ cup chicken stock

1 tablespoon of olive oil

Salt and pepper, to taste

2 tablespoons crispy bacon bits

1 tablespoon of chopped parsley

DIRECTIONS:

1. Place the inner cooking pot in the rice cooker, turn on and press the white rice button to start cooking. Add the oil and sauté the garlic until lightly brown and aromatic.

2. Add the lentils and carrots in the inner pot and cook for 2 minutes while stirring regularly. Pour in ½ cup stock and season to taste with salt and pepper. Close lid and bring to a boil. Switch to keep warm mode and let it cook with low heat for 10 minutes. Remove the inner cooking pot from the rice cooker.

3. Portion vegetables on individual serving bowls and serve warm with crispy bacon bits and parsley leaves on top.

European
Side Dish Recipes

ITALIAN-STYLE SWISS CHARD FRITTATA

Preparation time: 10 minutes

Cooking time: 10 to 15 minutes

Yields: 4

INGREDIENTS:

6 large whole eggs

¼ teaspoon salt, to taste

½ teaspoon freshly cracked black pepper

1 cup Swiss chard, trimmed and blanched

1 tablespoon of olive oil

1 ripe red onion, diced

1 teaspoon dried basil leaves

1 cup grated Pecorino Romano cheese

DIRECTIONS:

1. Whisk the eggs in a mixing bowl until foamy. Stir in the Swiss chard, cheese and cracked black pepper.

2. Place the inner cooking pot in the rice cooker, turn on and press the white rice button to start cooking. Add the oil and pour in the egg mixture, close lid and cook for about 6 to 8 minutes. Gently lift the frittata to allow the uncooked mixture to drizzle down and close lid, switch to keep warm mode and cook for 15 to 20 minutes, or until the eggs are set and cooked through.

3. Remove the inner cooking pot from the rice cooker. Place a plate on top and carefully turn it upside down to remove the frittata.

4. Serve immediately with extra basil leaves and grated cheese on top.

MEDITERRANEAN KALE

Preparation time: 15 minutes

Cooking time: 10 minutes

Yields: 3 to 4

INGREDIENTS:

6 cups chopped kale

1 tablespoon lemon juice

1 tablespoon olive oil, or as needed

1 teaspoon minced garlic

1 teaspoon soy sauce

salt to taste

ground black pepper to taste

DIRECTIONS:

1. Add a cup of water in the inner cooking pot, and then place the inner cooking pot in the rice cooker. Turn on and press the white rice button to start cooking. Close the lid and bring to a boil.

2. Place the kale on the steam tray, place the steam tray on the inner cooking pot, close the lid and steam kale for 8 to 10 minutes.

3. While steaming the kale, whisk together the soy sauce, lemon juice, oil, garlic, salt and pepper in a mixing bowl until the salt is completely dissolved.

4. When the kale is done, remove from the rice cooker and transfer into the bowl with the dressing. Toss to coat and transfer on a serving dish. Serve warm.

CLASSIC GREEK SPINACH

Preparation time: 30 minutes

Cooking time: 40 hour

Yields: 6

INGREDIENTS:

1 cup of extra virgin olive oil

½ cup of diced onions

1 cup tightly packed spinach

2 medium ripe red tomatoes, diced

3 cups chicken stock, or as needed

1 garlic clove, minced

2 tablespoons of tomato paste

salt and pepper to taste

½ cup uncooked long-grain white rice, rinsed and drained

DIRECTIONS:

1. Place the inner cooking pot in the rice cooker, turn on and press the white rice button to start cooking. Add the oil and sauté the onion and garlic until soft fragrant. Stir in the spinach and tomatoes and cook until the spinach is wilted and the tomatoes are tender.

2. Pour in 2 cups of stock, season to taste with salt and pepper. Add the tomato paste, close the lid and cook for about 15 minutes.

3. Add the rice and remaining stock, close lid and cook for another 20 minutes, or until the rice is cooked through and fluffy.

4.   Remove the inner cooking pot from the rice cooker. Transfer rice and spinach into individual serving bowls. Serve warm.

Sautéed Swiss Chard with Parmesan Cheese

Preparation time: 15 minutes

Cooking time: 10 minutes

Yields: 2 to 3

INGREDIENTS:

2 tablespoons unsalted butter

2 tablespoons extra virgin olive oil

1 garlic clove, minced

1 small red onion, diced

2 cups loosely packed Swiss chard, trimmed and chopped

½ cup of dry white wine

½ lemon, juiced, or as needed to taste

¼ cup Parmesan cheese, grated

Salt, to taste (optional)

DIRECTIONS:

1. Place the inner cooking pot in the rice cooker, turn on and press the white rice button to start cooking. Melt in the butter and sauté the garlic and onion for 1 minute, or until soft and fragrant.

2. Stir in the Swiss chard, lemon juice and the wine, season to taste with salt. Close lid and cook for 5 minutes, or until the Swiss chard is almost wilted. Switch to keep warm mode, stir the ingredients and maintain keep warm mode before serving.

3. Stir in the Parmesan cheese, portion Swiss chard on individual serving bowls, Serve immediately.

ITALIAN PEAS

Preparation time: 10 minutes

Cooking time: 40 to 45 minutes

Yields: 4 to 5

INGREDIENTS:

1 tablespoon of extra virgin olive oil

1 tablespoon ghee

3 shallot, minced

2 stalks of celery, diced

2 to 3 tablespoons of dry white wine

1 cup medium-grain starchy rice, soaked and drained

2 tablespoons medium-grain starchy rice

3 cups low sodium chicken stock

1 cup canned peas, drained

For serving

1 tablespoon butter

3 tablespoons of heavy cream

1⁄4 cup grated Parmesan cheese

DIRECTIONS:

1.   Place the inner cooking pot in the rice cooker, turn on and press the white rice button to start cooking. Add the oil and melt in the butter, sauté the shallots and celery until soft, or for 3 to 4

minutes. Pour in the wine and 1 cup of rice, briefly stir and cook for 3 minutes.

2. Add the peas and stock and then close the lid, cook for 30 minutes or until it switches to keep warm mode. Fluff the rice with the serving ladle and cook further id the rice is not yet cooked through.

3. Stir in the cheese, butter and the cream in the inner cooking pot and toss to coat. Close lid and cook for 10 minutes in keep warm mode.

4. Portion into individual serving bowls and serve immediately.

American
Side Dish Recipes

SUCCOTASH

Preparation time: 10 minutes

Cooking time: 25 minutes

Yields: 4

INGREDIENTS:

½ cup diced bacon

1 red onion, diced

1 teaspoon minced garlic cloves

4 ears of non-GMO corn, kernels cut off

1 large jalapeño, minced

1 cup baby lima beans

2 cups okra, cut into 1-inch pieces

1 cup cherry tomatoes, halved

2 tablespoons of white wine vinegar, or as needed to taste

¼ cup loosely packed fresh basil leaves, chopped

DIRECTIONS:

1. Place the bacon in the inner cooking pot. Place the inner pot in the rice cooker, turn on and press the white rice button to start cooking. Cook the bacon until crisp, remove with a slotted spoon and place on a plate with paper towels.

2. Sauté the onions in the inner cooking pot and cook until soft and translucent. Stir in the garlic and cook for 2 minutes while stirring regularly. Add the beans, okra, corn kernels, jalapeno and tomatoes, wine vinegar, basil, salt and black pepper and

close the lid. Cook for 20 minutes or until it switches to keep warm mode.

3. Portion succotash into individual serving dishes and serve warm with bacon bits on top.

STEWED OKRA & TOMATOES

Preparation time: 5 minutes

Cooking time: 30 minutes

Yields: 4

INGREDIENTS:

¼ cup crispy bacon bits

1 medium onion, chopped

1 pound okra, trimmed and cut into 1-inch pieces

1 cup canned diced tomatoes

Salt and coarsely ground black pepper, to taste

DIRECTIONS:

1. Place the inner cooking pot in the rice cooker, turn on and press the white rice button to start cooking.

2. Add the oil and sauté the onions until soft and translucent. Stir in the okras and tomatoes, season to taste with salt and pepper.

3. Close the lid and cook for 15 to 20 minutes. Mix in the bacon bits and stir briefly, close lid and switch to keep warm mode. Maintain keep warm mode before serving.

4. Transfer into individual serving dishes, serve warm with extra bacon bits on top.

MASHED POTATO

Preparation time: 15 minutes

Cooking time: 3 hours 15 minutes

Yields: 4 to 6

INGREDIENTS:

2 pounds red potatoes, cut into chunks

1 tablespoon minced garlic, or to taste

1 cube chicken bouillon

½ cup sour cream

½ cup cream cheese, softened

½ cup unsalted butter

Salt and ground pepper, to taste

DIRECTIONS:

1. Place the potatoes, garlic, chicken bouillon and salt in the inner cooking pot. Pour water just to cover the potatoes, turn on and press the white rice button to start cooking. Cook for 20 minutes and remove the potatoes with a slotted spoon, transfer the cooking liquid and set aside.

2. Mash the potatoes with a masher and mix in the cream cheese and sour cream. Add with enough cooking liquid until desired consistency is achieved.

3. Return the potato mixture into the inner pot, close and cook in keep warm mode for 2 hours. Stir in the butter just before serving.

4. Portion into individual serving bowls, adjust taste and serve warm.

CORN FRITTERS

Preparation time: 15 minutes

Cooking time: 20 to 25 minutes

Yields: 3 to 4

INGREDIENTS:

1/2 cup frozen whole-kernel corn, thawed

1/3 cup cooked rice

1 tablespoon all-purpose flour

1/2 teaspoon sugar

1/4 teaspoon baking powder

1/8 teaspoon salt

1/8 teaspoon black pepper

2 large eggs

2 tablespoons margarine or butter

DIRECTIONS:

1. Combine the corn, rice, flour, sugar, baking powder, salt, and black pepper in a mixing bowl and mix until well incorporated. Set aside.

2. Place the inner cooking pot in the rice cooker, turn on and add the butter. Set aside.

3. In small bowl, whisk the eggs until foamy. Fold in the egg in the inner cooking pot with the corn mixture.

4. Press the white rice button of the rice cooker and melt the butter. Take about half a cup of the corn mixture and shape it

into wide flat fritters, just enough to fit in the inner cooking pot. Close lid and cook for 3 minutes on each side, turn to cook the other side for 3 minutes. Repeat the procedure with the remaining ingredients.

5.   Transfer corn fritters on a serving dish and serve warm.

STEAMED CORN ON THE COB

Preparation time: 5 minutes

Cooking time: 20 minutes

Yields: 4

INGREDIENTS:

4 ears corn, husked and halved if needed to fit in the rice cooker

Water, as needed to fill line 1

2 tablespoons of salt

2 tablespoons butter, for serving

Ground black pepper, for serving

DIRECTIONS:

1. Add water to fill up to line 1 in the inner cooking pot, add salt and place the inner cooking pot in the rice cooker. Turn on and press the white rice button to start cooking. Bring water to a boil.

2. Place the corn on the steam tray and place it on the inner cooking pot, close lid and steam for about 15 minutes. Switch to keep warm mode and cook for 5 minutes more.

3. Remove the steam tray from rice cooker and cover with foil, until ready to serve.

4. Brush the corn with butter and season with salt and pepper, if preferred. Serve immediately.

8

SOUPS, STEWS AND CHILI

Popular Recipes

CREAMY POTATO SOUP

Preparation time: 15 minutes

Cooking time: 25 minutes

Yields: 6 to 8

INGREDIENTS:

2 cups of lean beef, ground

1 small white onion, diced

1 tablespoon cooking oil

1 large carrot, peeled and diced

1 medium stalk of celery, chopped

2 cups of beef stock

1 cup of water, or as needed

Salt and black pepper, to taste

3 Russet potatoes, peeled and cubed

½ cup of fresh milk

½ cup of cubed Cheddar Cheese, cubed

½ cup of canned evaporated milk

2 tablespoons chopped fresh parsley leaves

DIRECTIONS:

1. Place the inner cooking pot in the rice cooker, turn on and press the white rice button to start cooking. Add and heat in the oil, add the beef and cook until brown while stirring regularly. Stir in the onions, celery, and carrots and cook until soft and tender. Drain the excess fat, stir in the potatoes and pour in the stock.

Season to taste with salt and pepper, close the lid securely and cook until the potatoes are tender, or until the rice cooker switches to keep warm mode.

2. Stir in the cheese, milk and evaporated milk in the inner cooking pot and briefly stir to combine. Reset the rice cooker, close lid and return to a boil. Cook for about 10 minutes or until the sauce has thickened while stirring regularly.

3. Remove the inner cooking pot and portion soup into individual serving bowls. Serve warm with chopped parsley on top.

CLAM CHOWDER

Preparation time: 5 minutes

Cooking time: 35 minutes

Yields: 4 to 6

INGREDIENTS:

2 to 3 tablespoons of unsalted butter

2 medium onions, diced

1 medium stalk of celery, roughly chopped

2 to 3 garlic cloves, minced

2 medium white potatoes, peeled and cubed

2 tablespoons of flour

2 cups of vegetable or chicken stock

1 cup of cream

1 ½ cup of canned clams, drained and chopped

1 bay leaf

½ teaspoon of dried thyme

DIRECTIONS:

1. Place the inner cooking pot in the rice cooker, turn on and press the white rice button to start cooking. Melt in the butter and stir in the garlic, onions, and celery in the inner pot and sauté until soft and fragrant.

2. Slowly add the flour and cook until lightly brown while stirring constantly. Pour in the stock, and then add the thyme and

potatoes. Season to taste with salt and pepper, close lid and cook until the potatoes are tender, or for about 20 minutes.

3.   Stir in the clams and cream, cook for about 10 minutes or until the soup has returned to a boil. Remove the inner cooking pot from the rice cooker.

4.   Portion the soup into individual serving bowls and serve with your choice of bread.

FRENCH ONION SOUP

Preparation time: 10 minutes

Cooking time: 2 hours and 10 minutes

Yields: 8

INGREDIENTS:

3 white onions, sliced into rounds

¼ cup of clarified butter or melted butter

¼ cup of flour

1 to 2 tablespoons of Worcestershire sauce

½ tablespoon sugar

½ teaspoon of coarsely ground pepper

4 cups of beef stock

French bread, sliced into 8 1-inch thick slices

¾ to 1 cup of Mozzarella cheese, shredded

¼ cup of Parmesan cheese, grated

DIRECTIONS:

1. Place the inner cooking pot in the rice cooker, turn on and press the white rice button to start cooking. Add the clarified butter and the onions, cook for about 5 minutes or until the onions are soft and translucent. Stir in the flour, sugar, ground pepper and the Worcestershire sauce in the inner pot and cook for 5 minutes while stirring regularly. Pour in the stock, close the lid securely and cook for about 2 hours or until the rice cooker switches to keep warm mode.

2. When the onion very tender, prepare the bread for serving. Top each slice with Mozzarella and Parmesan cheese and set aside.

3. Portion onion soup into individual serving bowls and serve warm with a slice of bread on top.

PUMPKIN SOUP

Preparation time: 45 minutes

Cooking time: 2 to 3 hours

Yields: 4 to 6

INGREDIENTS:

1 pound of butternut squash, seeded and peeled, diced

1 large potato, peeled and diced

1 red onion, diced

½ tablespoon of curry powder

½ teaspoon of cayenne pepper

Salt and coarsely ground black pepper, to taste

2 to 3 cups of vegetable stock

1 cup of heavy cream

DIRECTIONS:

1.   In the inner cooking pot, add the stock, butternut squash, curry powder and the onions. Place the inner cooking pot in the rice cooker, turn on and press the white rice button. Close lid and cook until the squash is tender, or for about 2 to 3 hours. Remove the inner cooking pot from the rice cooker, let it rest to cool.

2.   Transfer the mixture into a food processor or blender and pulse until smooth and thick. Stir in the cream and cayenne pepper and briefly pulse to combine.

3. Before serving, reheat the soup in the rice cooker for about 5 minutes. Season to taste salt and pepper and portion soup into individual serving bowls. Serve immediately.

BEEF STEW

Preparation time: 10 minutes

Cooking time: 1 hour

Yields: 4

INGREDIENTS:

1 tablespoon of olive oil

1 pound of beef stew meat, cut into cubes

1 cup of tomato sauce

1 large onion, diced

2 medium red bell peppers, diced

1 medium stalk of celery, chopped

1 small carrot, peeled and diced

½ cup of canned peas, drained

1 medium potato, peeled and diced

½ cup of canned white beans, drained

2 garlic cloves, minced

½ cup of water, or as needed

DIRECTIONS:

1. Place the inner cooking pot in the rice cooker, turn on and press the white rice button to start cooking. Add the oil and heat until it start to smoke, add the half of beef and cook until browned on all sides. Remove from the inner pot and brown the remaining meat.

2. Return the browned beef and all of the remaining ingredients into the inner cooking pot. Cook for about 1 hour or until the beef is tender and the vegetables are soft. Stir the ingredients occasionally while cooking to avoid browning of contents on the bottom of the pot. Season beef stew to taste with salt and pepper and remove the inner cooking pot from the rice cooker.

3. Portion soup into individual serving bowls and serve warm.

Asian Recipes

CHINESE CHILI

Preparation time: 10 minutes

Cooking time: 2 hours

Yields: 6

INGREDIENTS:

1 pound of beef brisket, trimmed and cut into 1-inch cubes

3 tablespoons of light soy sauce

3 tablespoons of hoisin sauce

2 red onions, diced

1 tablespoon of oil

2 medium bell peppers, diced and seeded

1 to 2 jalapeños pepper, chopped

1 red hot chili pepper, chopped

3 garlic cloves, minced

1 tablespoon fresh ginger root, grated

2 to 3 teaspoons of crushed Sichuan pepper

2 to 3 teaspoons of five-spice mix

1 cup of beer

1 cup of canned diced tomatoes

2 to 3 teaspoons of cider vinegar

Chili oil, as needed of extra heat

¼ cup of loosely packed fresh cilantro, minced

DIRECTIONS:

1. Place the inner cooking pot into the rice cooker, turn on and press the white rice button and add the oil. Once the oil is hot, add the beef and cook until brown on all sides. Remove from the inner cooking pot and transfer to a bowl.

2. Pour in the hoisin sauce and light soy sauce in the bowl and toss to coat the beef with sauce.

3. Add the bell peppers, onions, chili, jalapeno, garlic and ginger in the inner cooking pot and cook for about 5 minutes, or until the vegetables are soft and aromatic. Stir in the crushed Sichuan peppers, five-spice mix and tomatoes and then pour in the beer. Close the lid and cook for about 1 ½ hour or until the beef is tender.

4. Pour in the cider vinegar and add more water if the soup is too thick. Stir in the chili oil and adjust seasoning by adding salt and soy sauce. Once the beef is tender, remove the inner cooking pot from heat.

5. Portion into individual serving bowls and serve warm with chopped cilantro on top.

MISO SOUP

Preparation time: 5 minutes

Cooking time: 15 to 20 minutes

Yields: 4

INGREDIENTS:

4 cups Dashi stock

3 to 4 tablespoons of miso paste

1 to 1 ½ cup of silken tofu, cubed

2 medium spring onions, cut into ½-inch bias cuts

DIRECTIONS:

1. Add the Dashi stock in the inner cooking pot and place into the rice cooker. Turn on the rice cooker, press the white rice button and bring the stock to a boil. Stir in the miso paste and tofu, return to a boil and add the spring onions. Remove inner cooking pot from the rice cooker.

2. Portion miso soup into individual serving bowls. Serve immediately.

CURRY LAKSA

Preparation time: 15 minutes

Cooking time: 1 hour

Yields: 4 to 6

INGREDIENTS:

3 to 4 tablespoons of ghee or vegetable oil

2 to 3 tablespoon of laksa paste

4 cups of chicken stock

1 tablespoon raw cane sugar

1 pound of chicken thighs, debones and skinned, cut into bite size pieces

½ pound of fresh prawns (with tails), peeled and deveined

2 cups of fresh or canned coconut milk

1 cup of fried tofu, sliced

2 cups of fresh bean sprouts

1 pound of raw rice noodles

fried Asian shallots (see Note),

2 tablespoons fresh mint leaves, for serving

Chili Sambal, for serving

Lime wedges, for serving

DIRECTIONS:

1. Place the inner cooking pot into the rice cooker, turn on and press the white rice button to start cooking. Add the oil, stir in 2 tablespoons of laksa paste and cook for about 2 minutes or until fragrant while stirring regularly. Add the sugar, chicken and

stock in the inner pot, and then cook until the chicken is cooked through. Stir in the prawns and cook for 3 minutes or until the prawns are half cooked.

2. Stir in the coconut milk, tofu and bean sprouts, and then bring to a gentle boil. Switch to keep warm mode.

3. While cooking the soup with low heat, place the rice noodles in a large bowl and pour in enough boiling water just cover. Let it stand for 3 minutes or until the rice noodles have softened. Drain and set aside.

4. Portion noodles into individual serving bowls, top with fried shallots and mint. Add ½ teaspoon of chili sambal on top and pour in the laksa soup. Serve immediately with lime wedges.

CHICKEN NOODLE SOUP

Preparation time: 15 minutes

Cooking time: 25 minutes

Yields: 6

INGREDIENTS:

1 tablespoon of ghee or melted butter

1 medium stalk of celery, chopped

1 large carrot, peeled and diced

1 large onion diced

1 potato, peeled and diced

1 teaspoon of dried thyme

½ tablespoon of poultry seasoning

4 cups of chicken stock

½ to 1 cup of egg noodles

2 cups of roasted or boiled chicken, shredded or chopped

Fresh parsley leaves, for serving

DIRECTIONS:

1. Place the inner cooking pot into the rice cooker, turn and press the white rice button. Add the ghee, onions, celery and carrots in the inner pot and cook until soft and fragrant.

2. Add the potatoes, dried thyme, poultry seasoning and stock into the inner pot. Close the lid, bring it to a boil and cook until the potatoes are tender.

3.   Stir in the chicken and noodles, close the lid and cook for about 20 minutes, or until the noodles have soft. Switch to keep warm mode before serving.

4.   Portion noodles and soup into individual serving bowls. Serve immediately with fresh parsley leaves on top.

BHO KHO

Preparation time: 20 minutes

Cooking time: 2 to 3 hours on low

Yields: 4 to 6

INGREDIENTS:

1 pound of beef shank, cut into 1-inch cubes

1-inch fresh ginger root, sliced into rounds

1 medium stalk of lemongrass, white part (bruised) and green leaves (tied)separated

1 bay leaf

2 star anise seeds

3 cups of beef stock

2 large carrots, peeled and chopped

½ tablespoon annatto seed oil

Lime wedges, for serving

Diced cilantro or green onions, for serving

Sliced jalapenos, for serving

Fresh Basil, for serving

For the Marinade

1 shallot, minced

2 garlic cloves, minced

1 teaspoon smoked paprika

1-inch lemongrass (white part), minced

2 to 3 teaspoons of fish sauce

1 pinch of red chili powder, or as needed for extra heat

1 pinch of ground cinnamon

1 pinch of ground clove

1 pinch of ground anise

Ground black pepper and sugar, to taste

DIRECTIONS:

1. Combine together all ingredients for the marinade in a large bowl and mix it thoroughly. Add the beef and toss to coat evenly with the marinade. Let it stand for at least 1 hour.

2. Place the inner cooking pot into the rice cooker, turn on and press the white rice button to start cooking. Add the annatto seed oil and heat until it starts to smoke, add the beef and brown on all sides. Stir in the bruised lemongrass, star anise seeds, bay leaf and pour in the stock in the inner pot. Add more stock if needed to just to cover the meat, close lid and bring to a boil.

3. Cook until the beef is tender, or until the rice cooker switches to keep warm mode. Reset the rice cooker if the beef is not yet ready if it has switched to keep warm mode. If the beef is almost done, maintain keep warm mode for another hour or more.

4. An hour before serving the soup, add the carrots, annatto seed oil and season to taste with black pepper, salt and sugar.

5. Portion into individual serving bowls and serve immediately with preferred toppings.

Middle Eastern Recipes

LENTIL SOUP

Preparation time: 30 minutes

Cooking time: 45 minutes

Yields: 6

INGREDIENTS:

1 to 2 tablespoons of cooking oil

2 medium onions, diced

1 medium carrot, peeled and diced

1 medium stalk celery, chopped

½ tablespoon of salt, or as needed to taste

2 cups lentils, rinsed and drained

1 cup tomatoes, prepared into concasse and diced

4 cups of chicken stock

1/2 teaspoon freshly ground coriander

1/2 teaspoon freshly ground toasted cumin

1/2 teaspoon freshly ground grains of paradise

DIRECTIONS:

1. Place the inner cooking pot into the rice cooker, turn on and press the white rice button to start cooking. Add and heat the oil until it starts to smoke, sauté the onions, celery, carrots and salt until soft and fragrant. Stir in the lentils, coriander, tomatoes, cumin and the stock. Close the lid, bring to a boil and cook until the lentils are tender. Switch to keep warm mode and wait for about 10 minutes before removing the inner pot from the cooker.

2. Let it stand to lower in temperature and transfer into a food processor or blender, pulse until smooth or into a coarse mixture.

3. Portion into individual serving bowls and serve immediately.

MOROCCAN LENTIL STEW WITH RAISINS

Preparation time: 15 minutes

Cooking time: 2 hours

Yields: 4

INGREDIENTS:

1 to 2 tablespoons of cooking oil

1 white onion, finely diced

1 cup canned chickpeas

4 cups of vegetable stock

2 garlic cloves, minced

1 tablespoon fresh cilantro, chopped

1 teaspoon table salt

2 medium stalk of celery, chopped

2 red tomatoes, diced

½ cup lentils, rinsed

1 teaspoon tomato paste

1 teaspoon lemon juice

1 cinnamon stick

1 pinch sweet paprika

1 pinch turmeric

1/2 teaspoon grated ginger

1 pinch coriander powder

1 pinch nutmeg

1 pinch ground pepper

1 pinch clove powder

½ cup vermicelli, broken into pieces

½ cup of dates, pitted and chopped

¼ cup loosely packed fresh parsley leaves, plus whole leaves for garnish

lemon wedges , for serving

DIRECTIONS:

1.   Place the inner cooking pot into the rice cooker, turn and press the white rice button. Add the oil and sauté the onions for 5 minutes or until soft and tender. Stir in the chickpeas and pour in the stock. Close the lid and cook for about 30 minutes.

2.   Add the garlic, cilantro, celery, tomatoes, lentils, lemon juice, tomato paste, and ground spices into the pot. Close the lid and cook for 30 minutes.

3.   Stir in the vermicelli and dates and cook for about 10 minutes or until the noodles have softened. Stir in extra chopped cilantro and parsley, and then remove the inner pot from the rice cooker.

4.   Portion into individual serving bowls and serve immediately with lemon wedges.

MOROCCAN CHICKPEA CHILI

Preparation time: 20 minutes

Cooking time: 20 minutes

Yields: 4

INGREDIENTS:

½ tablespoon oil

1 medium onion, diced

1 medium stalk celery, chopped

1 small carrot, diced

½ teaspoon minced garlic

1 teaspoon cumin

1 teaspoon smoked paprika

1-inch fresh ginger root, grated

½ teaspoon turmeric powder

1 pinch black pepper

1 pinch salt

1 pinch cinnamon powder

½ teaspoon crushed red pepper flakes

1 cup of water

3 tablespoons unsalted tomato paste

2 cups canned chickpeas, drained

1 cup canned diced tomatoes

¼ cup loosely packed fresh cilantro leaves, chopped

2 to 3 teaspoons of lemon juice

DIRECTIONS:

1. Place the inner cooking pot into the rice cooker, turn on and press the white rice button. Add the oil and heat until it starts to smoke. Sauté the onions, garlic, celery, carrots for5 minutes or until soft and fragrant while stirring occasionally.

2. Add the ground spices, briefly stir and season with salt and pepper. Stir in the tomato paste, tomatoes, and chickpeas and pour in the water. Close the lid and bring it to a boil. Switch to keep warm mode and cook with low heat until the chickpeas are tender. Stir in the cilantro and lemon juice and remove the inner cooking pot from the rice cooker.

3. Portion into individual serving bowls and serve warm.

MIDDLE EASTERN LAMB STEW

Preparation time: 40 minutes

Cooking time: 3 hours to 30 minutes to 4 hours

Yields: 4 to 6

INGREDIENTS:

1 pound lamb stew meat, cut into 1-inch cubes

1 tablespoon canola oil

½ tablespoon cumin powder

1 teaspoon coriander powder

1 pinch cayenne pepper

1 pinch of salt

Freshly ground pepper, to taste

1 medium onion, diced

½ cup canned diced tomatoes

½ cup chicken stock

1 garlic clove, minced

½ cup canned chickpeas, rinsed

½ cup loosely packed baby spinach

DIRECTIONS:

1. Combine together the oil, cayenne, cumin, salt and pepper in a bowl and mix until well combined. Set aside.

2. Place the inner cooking pot into the rice cooker, add the meat and turn on the rice cooker. Pour in the spice mixture, toss to

coat the meat with the mixture and press the white rice button. Add the onions on top, tomatoes, garlic and pour in the stock. Close the lid and cook until the meat is tender, if the rice cooker switches to keep warm mode and the meat is not yet done, reset and continue cooking.

3. When the lamb is tender, stir in the chickpeas and spinach and cook until the spinach is wilted. Remove the inner pot from the rice cooker.

4. Portion meat and vegetables into individual serving bowls and serve immediately.

TOMATO AND CHICKPEA SOUP

Preparation time: 5 minutes

Cooking time: 25 minutes

Yields: 4

INGREDIENTS:

1 tablespoon cooking oil

1 red onion, diced

1 medium stalk celery, diced

½ tablespoon cumin

2 cups vegetable stock

1 cup canned plum tomatoes, diced

1 cup canned chickpeas, drained

½ cup broad beans

½ lemon, juiced and zested

½ cup loosely packed fresh coriander leaves, for serving

DIRECTIONS:

1. Place the inner cooking pot into the rice cooker, turn on and press the white rice button. Add the oil and sauté the onions and celery for 5 minutes or until soft and tender. Stir in the cumin, stir to combine and cook for 1 minute.

2. Stir in the tomatoes, chickpeas, broad beans, black pepper and pour in the stock with the lemon juice. Bring to a boil and cook for about 10 minutes or until the beans and chickpeas are tender.

3.   Switch to keep warm mode and add the lemon zest and herbs, remove inner pot form the rice cooker.

4.   Portion into individual serving bowls and serve immediately.

European
Recipes

CHICKEN SOUP WITH EGG-LEMON SAUCE

Preparation time: 15 minutes

Cooking time: 1 hour 20 minutes

Yields: 4 to 6

INGREDIENTS:

½ whole chicken, chopped into pieces

2 cups water

½ teaspoon salt

1 medium leek, cleaned and quartered

1 small carrot, peeled and quartered

1 bay leaf

1 tablespoons extra-virgin olive oil

½ cup diced onions

½ cup short-grain rice, rinsed and drained

2 tablespoons lemon juice

1 large egg

½ teaspoon freshly ground pepper

DIRECTIONS:

1. Place the chicken, salt and water in the inner cooking pot and place the inner pot into the rice cooker. Turn on the rice cooker, press the white rice button and bring to a boil. Close the lid and cook for about 30 minutes or until the chicken is cooked through.

2.   Skim the foam from the surface and add the leek, bay leaf and carrots. Close the lid, cook for 30 another 30 minutes or until the vegetables are tender. Remove the chicken with a slotted spoon and set aside to cool, strain the stock and place into a bowl. Set aside.

3.   Remove the bones and skin of the chicken and cut into cubes.

4.   Return the inner cooking pot into the rice cooker, press the white rice button and add the oil. Once the oil is hot, sauté the onions and cook until soft and translucent. Stir in the chicken and rice, sauté for 1 minute and pour in the strained stock. Close the lid and cook for about 20 minutes or until the rice is cooked through.

5.   While cooking the rice, whisk together the eggs, lemon juice and pepper in a mixing bowl. Stir in 1 cup of hot stock while whisking constantly. Pour the egg mixture into the pot, stir to combine and season to taste with salt. Switch to keep warm mode and cook with low heat before serving.

6.   Portion the soup into individual serving bowls and serve immediately.

ITALIAN SAUSAGE SOUP

Preparation time: 15 minutes

Cooking time: 3 hours 15 minutes

Yields: 4 to 6

INGREDIENTS:

½ pound sweet Italian sausage, casings remove and chopped

1 garlic clove, minced

1 medium onion, diced

1 cup of canned whole tomatoes

½ cup dry red wine

2 cups of beef stock

¼ teaspoon dried basil

¼ teaspoon dried oregano

1 medium zucchini, sliced into rounds

1 green bell pepper, chopped

2 tablespoons of fresh parsley leaves, chopped

½ cu fettuccine pasta

Salt and black pepper, to taste

DIRECTIONS:

1. Add 2 cups of water and ¼ teaspoon in the inner cooking pot and place into the rice cooker. Turn on the rice cooker, press the white rice button and bring to a boil. Add the past and cook for about 5 minutes or until al dente. Strain the pasta, place into a bowl and set aside.

2. Place the sausage into the inner cooking pot. Place the inner pot into the rice cooker, turn on and press the white rice button to cook the sausage until brown. Remove the sausage with a slotted spoon, reserve 1 tablespoon of cooking fat and drain the excess fat.

3. Add the reserved cooking fat into the inner pot, add the onions and garlic and cook soft and translucent. Return the sausage and stir in the bell pepper, zucchini, tomatoes, red wine, stock, basil, oregano and parsley. Close lid, season to taste with salt and pepper and cook for about 30 minutes, or until vegetables are soft. Stir in the pasta and cook until it returns to a boil. Switch to keep warm mode, and keep it warm before serving.

4. Portion the soup into individual serving bowls and serve immediately.

SPANISH CHICKPEA AND CHORIZO SOUP

Preparation time: 15 minutes

Cooking time: 1 hour

Yields: 3 to 4

INGREDIENTS:

1 tablespoon of cooking oil

½ cup diced onions

½ tablespoon minced garlic

½ cup diced Spanish chorizo

2 cups of chicken stock

1 cup of canned chickpeas, drained

1 bay leaf

2 cups chopped escarole

2 teaspoons sherry vinegar

½ teaspoon table salt

½ teaspoon black pepper, coarsely ground

1 pinch of red pepper flakes, crushed

DIRECTIONS:

1. Place the inner cooking pot into the rice cooker and add the oil, place the inner cooking pot into the rice cooker and turn it on. Press the white rice button and heat the oil. Once the oil is hot, sauté the onions until soft and stir in the chorizo and garlic. Sauté the ingredients until the chorizo are lightly browned and add in the chickpeas, bay leaf and the stock. Close the lid, cook

for about 30 minutes or until the meat and chickpeas are thoroughly cooked.

2. Open the rice cooker and open the lid, remove and discard the bay leaf and add in the escarole and remaining ingredients. Close the lid, cook until the escarole is wilted and the soup has returned to a boil. Switch and maintain to keep warm mode before serving.

3. Portion the soup into individual serving bowls and serve immediately.

CALLOS CON GARBANZOS

Preparation time: 20 minutes

Cooking time: 1 to 2 hours

Yields: 3 to 4

INGREDIENTS:

1 cup of honeycomb tripe, boiled ahead

1 cup of cooked beef strips

1 cup of beef stock

2 tablespoons of olive oil

1 teaspoon of annatto powder

½ link of chorizo de Bilbao, sliced into thin rounds

1 teaspoon of minced garlic

1 small onion, diced

½ cup of chopped sun dried tomatoes in oil

1 red chili, chopped

¼ cup loosely packed fresh oregano, chopped

1 small potatoes, peeled and cubes

1 small carrot, peeled and diced

1 bell pepper, seeded and cut into strips

¼ cup canned peas, drained

¼ cup of canned chickpeas, drained

Salt, sugar and black pepper, to taste

DIRECTIONS:

1. Add the oil in the inner cooking pot and the place the inner pot into the rice cooker. Turn on the rice cooker, press the white rice button and heat the oil. Add the chorizo and cook for about 2 minutes while stirring regularly. Add in the garlic, onions, tomatoes, annatto powder, chili and oregano into the pot and sauté for 2 minutes until fragrant.

2. Add in the beef, tripe, carrots, potatoes, peas, chickpeas and bell peppers into the inner cooking pot and pour in the stock. Season to taste with salt, sugar and black pepper, close the lid and cook for about 1 hour or until the sauce has reduced and the ingredients are tender. If the rice cooker has switched to keep warm mode and the meat and tripe are not yet done, reset and press the white rice button to continue cooking.

3. Stir the ingredients occasionally while cooking. Switch to keep warm mode and cook for 30 minutes with low heat. Add more stock if the sauce is too thick and adjust seasoning. Maintain keep warm mode before serving.

4. Portion into individual serving bowls and serve immediately with rice or crusty bread.

OXTAIL SOUP

Preparation time: 15 minutes

Cooking time: 2 to 3 hours

Yields: 4

INGREDIENTS:

1 pound oxtail, chopped

1 teaspoon of Italian seasoning mix

½ tablespoon of olive oil

1 cup of beef stock

3 tablespoons of red wine

1 teaspoon of Worcestershire sauce

2 garlic cloves, chopped

½ teaspoon of dried basil leaves

½ teaspoon of dried oregano leaves

1 bay leaf

½ cup canned tomato sauce

1 white onion, cut into wedges

2 small red potatoes, cut in ½-inch cubes

1 medium carrot, cut into sticks

DIRECTIONS:

1. Season the oxtail with Italian seasoning evenly on all sides. Set aside.

2. Add the oil in the inner cooking pot and place the inner pot in to the rice cooker. Turn on the rice cooker, press the white rice button and heat the oil. Add the oxtail and brown on all sides while turning occasionally to evenly cook on all sides. Remove from the inner pot and set aside.

3. Add the stock, red wine, onions, garlic and Worcestershire sauce into the pot and cook for 1 minute while scraping the brown bits from the bottom. Stir in the oregano, basil, bay leaf, tomato sauce, in the inner cooking pot and return the oxtail. Stir to combine, close lid and cook for about 1 hour and 30 minutes or until the oxtail is done. Reset the rice cooker if it has switched to keep warm mode and the oxtail is not yet done.

4. Once the oxtail is done add the onion wedges, carrots, and potatoes and cook for about 15 minutes or until the vegetables are tender. Switch to keep warm mode, and maintain low steady to continue cooking the oxtail until very tender.

5. Transfer soup into a serving bowl and serve immediately.

American Recipes

SEAFOOD CHOWDER

Preparation time: 10 minutes

Cooking time: 40 minutes

Yields: 4

INGREDIENTS:

½ pound of ling cod fillets, sliced into bite size pieces

½ cup diced bell pepper

½ cup diced stalk of celery

½ cup of diced white onions

½ cup of canned tomatoes

½ cup of tomato sauce

1 tablespoon of unsalted butter

1 tablespoon of minced fresh parsley

Salt and black pepper, to taste

1 cup white cooked long-grain rice, rinsed

DIRECTIONS:

1. Add the butter in the inner cooking pot and place the inner pot into the rice cooker. Turn on the rice cooker and press the white rice button to melt the butter. Sauté the onions, celery, and bell pepper until soft and fragrant. Stir in the parsley, tomatoes and tomato sauce and cook for 3 minutes while stirring occasionally.

2. Add the fish into the inner cooking pot, briefly stir to combine and close the lid. Bring to a boil and cook until the sauce has thickened. Switch to keep warm mode and cook with low heat

until the fish is thoroughly cooked. Season to taste with salt and pepper.

3. Portion the rice into individual serving bowls, top with fish and pour over the sauce. Serve immediately.

Brazilian Salt Cod Stew

Preparation time: 10 minutes

Cooking time: 55 to 60 minutes

Yields: 6

INGREDIENTS:

½ pound salt cod fillets, soaked overnight and rinsed

½ cup of olive oil

½ cup of milk

1 large white onions, sliced into rounds

1 large potato, peeled

3 hard-boiled eggs, quartered

¼ cup of green olives, quartered

Salt and coarsely ground black pepper, to taste

DIRECTIONS:

1. Place the salt cod pieces into the inner cooking pot and pour with milk to cover. Place the inner cooking pot into the rice cooker, turn on and press the white rice button. Close the lid and bring it to a boil. Switch to keep warm mode and cook until the fish is tender. Remove the fish with a slotted spoon and transfer into a bowl. Set aside.

2. Add the potatoes into the pot, close the lid and cook for about 20 minutes or until tender. Remove potatoes and slice into thin rounds, and then pour the milk into a bowl. Set aside.

3. Wash the inner cooking pot and wipe with cloth. Return into the rice cooker and coat the bottom with oil. Press the white rice

button and layer the onions on the bottom. Place the potato on top of the onions, break the fish into small pieces and place it over the potatoes.

4. Add the olives and then the quartered eggs, pour with generous amounts of olive oil. Season to taste with salt and black pepper. Close the lid and bring it to a boil. Switch to keep warm mode and cook for 30 minutes, or until the ingredients are cooked through. Maintain keep warm mode before serving.

5. Transfer into a serving bowl and serve immediately.

PUCHERO

Preparation time: 25 minutes

Cooking time: 1 hour 30 minutes

Yields: 4

INGREDIENTS:

1 smoked ham bone

1 cup cooked chicken meat, cut into bite size pieces

½ cup pork belly

1 cup of beef bone broth

½ cup canned chickpeas, drained

1 medium stalk of celery, chopped

1 carrot, peeled and diced

1 tablespoon apple cider vinegar

1 turnip, diced

1 medium leek, chopped

1 red onion, diced or quartered

1 medium potato, peeled and diced

½ head of medium green cabbage, chopped

I head of pak choi, chopped

DIRECTIONS:

1. Place meat and bones into the inner cooking pot, together with the chickpeas, celery, carrots, leek, turnip and the onions. Add water to fill 2 inches above the ingredients.

2.   Stir in the cider vinegar and close the lid, turn on the rice cooker and press the white rice button. Bring to a boil, skim off the foam that floats on the surface and close the lid. Cook for about 1 hour or until the chickpeas are tender and the bones has released most of its flavors.

3.   Stir in the potatoes and cook for 20 minutes, or until the potatoes are tender. Remove the meat and bones with a slotted spoon and place into a bowl. Strain the broth to separate the vegetables and add into the bowl.

4.   Return the strained stock into the inner cooking pot and return to a boil. Add the pak choi and cabbage and cook until wilted, season to taste with salt and pepper.

5.   Portion soup and leafy vegetables into individual serving bowls and top with the meat.

ARGENTINE HOMINY STEW

Preparation time: 10 minutes

Cooking time: 45 minutes

Yields: 4

INGREDIENTS:

1 cup of cooked long-grain rice

1 ½ cups of water

1 teaspoons of salt

1 cup of sliced fresh cut okra

2 cups of chicken stock

1 cup canned hominy, drained

1 jalapeno pepper, finely chopped

Black pepper, coarsely ground to taste

1 teaspoon of crushed cumin seeds

1 cup of sliced pork tenderloin

1 teaspoon of olive oil

2 tablespoons fresh cilantro leaves, finely chopped

DIRECTIONS:

1. Combine together the crushed cumin, ¼ teaspoon of black pepper and salt in a bowl and add the meat. Toss to coat the meat evenly with the spice mixture.

2. Place the inner cooking pot into the rice cooker, press the white rice button and coat with oil. Once the oil is hot, add the meat and brown for 1 minute on each side or until the meat is no

longer pink. Remove from the inner pot and slice into thin strips. Set aside.

3. Add the stock into the inner cooking pot, place the inner pot into the rice cooker and turn it on. Press the white rice button, close the lid and bring the stock to a boil. When the stock reaches to a boil, stir in the cooked rice, okra, jalapeno, hominy, salt and pepper. When the stock returns to a boil, switch the rice cooker to keep warm mode. Simmer for 20 minutes or until okra is tender.

4. Portion the soup and vegetables into individual serving bowls and top with thin slices of pork meat.

ALL-AMERICAN CHILI RECIPE

Preparation time: 10 minutes

Cooking time: 40 to 45 minutes

Yields: 6 to 8

INGREDIENTS:

2 links of Turkey Italian sausage, casing removed and chopped

1 cup of diced onions

½ cup of diced bell pepper

2 teaspoons of minced garlic

½ pound of ground sirloin

1 jalapeño pepper, chopped

1 to 2 tablespoons of red chili powder

1 tablespoon of brown sugar

2 teaspoons cumin powder

2 tablespoon of tomato paste

½ teaspoon oregano, dried

½ teaspoon black pepper, coarsely ground

2 pinches salt

1 bay leaf

½ cup red wine

1 cup canned tomatoes, chopped

1 cup canned kidney beans, drained

½ cup of Cheddar cheese, grated

DIRECTIONS:

1. Place the inner cooking pot into the rice cooker, turn on and press the white rice button. Add the oil and sausage, cook for 5 minutes or until browned while stirring occasionally. Stir in the onions, ground beef, bell pepper, garlic and jalapeno into the inner pot and cook for about 5 minutes while stirring occasionally.

2. Stir in the chili powder, sugar, cumin, oregano, black pepper, sugar, salt, bay leaf and tomato paste. Cook for 1 minute and stir in the tomatoes, red wine and beans into the inner pot. Close the lid and bring to a boil. Cook for 30 minutes and switch to keep warm mode. Let it cook for 30 minutes with low heat or until the ingredients are tender and cooked through.

3. Open lid and press the white rice button, remove and discard the bay leaf. Cook for 10 minutes and switch to keep warm mode, remove the inner cooking pot from the rice cooker and stir in the cheese.

4. Portion chili into individual serving bowls and serve warm.

9

MAIN COURSES

Popular Main Course Recipes

ROASTED PORK

Preparation time: 10 minutes

Cooking time: 2 hours to 2 hours 30 minutes

Yields: 8

INGREDIENTS:

2 ½-pound of pork butt

½ cup loosely packed scallions

1-inch fresh ginger root, sliced into rounds

4 garlic cloves, crushed

Salt and coarsely ground black pepper, to taste

1 tablespoon of cooking oil

½ cup of light soy sauce

½ cup packed sugar

½ cup of hoisin sauce

DIRECTIONS:

1. Season the meat with generous amounts of salt and pepper and rub on all sides. Tie with a kitchen twine to retain a round form when cooked.

2. Place the inner cooking pot into the rice cooker, turn on and press the white rice button. Coat the bottom of the pan with oil and add the meat when the oil is hot. Add the garlic and brown the meat on all sides while turning to cook the other side.

3. Add in the ginger, scallions, sugar, soy sauce and hoisin sauce and slowly stir the ingredients to combine. Baste the meat with

sauce occasionally while cooking, and turn to cook the other side. Close the lid, cook until the sauce has thickened and switch to keep warm mode to simmer. If the meat is not yet done, reset the rice cooker and add ¼ cup of stock or red wine to avoid the sauce from burning. Check regularly and switch to keep warm mode when the meat is thoroughly cooked.

4. When the twisting action of the fork inserted in the meat is effortless or the meat flakes or shreds easily, the meat is already done. Remove the meat from the inner cooking pot, transfer to a plate and cover with foil. Let it stand for 10 minutes before serving.

5. Transfer the meat into a serving dish and drizzle the sauce on top. Serve immediately.

BEEF STEAK

Preparation time: 5 minutes

Cooking time: 10 to 15 minutes

Yields: 1

INGREDIENTS:

1 piece beef steak (1 cm thick)

Salt and crushed black pepper, to taste

4 asparagus spears, trimmed

1 tablespoon butter

DIRECTIONS:

1.   Place the inner cooking pot into the rice cooker, turn on and press the white rice button. Melt the butter in the inner pot and add the asparagus. Season with salt and pepper and sauté for about 4 minutes while turning to cook evenly. Remove from the inner cooking pot, place into a plate and set aside.

2.   Season the steak with salt and crushed black pepper on both sides. Place it in the inner cooking pot and briefly sear for about 30 seconds on each side. Close the lid and switch to keep warm mode. Cook for 5 minutes on each side with low heat, turn to cook the other side for another 5 minutes. After cooking in keep warm mode, remove from the inner cooking pot and transfer on a plate.

3.   Before serving the meat, reheat briefly in the rice cooker with the juices on the plate. Remove from the inner pot, transfer on a serving plate and serve with the asparagus spears.

HONEY GLAZED CHICKEN

Preparation time: 5 minutes

Cooking time: 35 minutes

Yields: 4

INGREDIENTS:

2 chicken breast fillets

½ cup of local honey

3 tablespoons of light soy sauce

1 small onion, diced

2 tablespoons of tomato paste

2 teaspoons of cooking oil

1 garlic clove, minced

1 teaspoon ginger powder

½ teaspoon of crushed red pepper flakes

DIRECTIONS:

1. Combine together all ingredients except for the chicken in a bowl. Mix the ingredients thoroughly and add the chicken, toss to coat the meat evenly with the sauce. Add into the inner cooking pot and place the inner pot into the rice cooker. Turn on the rice cooker, close the lid and press the white rice button.

2. Cook the chicken for 30 minutes, or until the rice cooker switches to keep warm mode. Turn the chicken after the 15 minutes of cooking. Reset the rice cooker if the chicken is yet done and add 1 tablespoon of water. Before serving, maintain

keep warm mode to make the chicken more flavorful and tenderer.

3. Remove the chicken from the inner pot, transfer on a cutting board and when cooled chop into small pieces. Return into the inner cooking pot and toss to coat the meat evenly.

4. Transfer to a serving dish and serve immediately.

BEEF BROCCOLI

Preparation time: 10 minutes

Cooking time: 1 hour

Yields: 4

INGREDIENTS:

1 cup of beef stock

3 tablespoons of light soy sauce

3 tablespoons of oyster sauce

3 tablespoon of sugar

2 to 3 teaspoons of toasted sesame oil

2 garlic cloves, minced

½ pound of thinly sliced beef tenderloin

1 tablespoon of corn starch

1 large head of broccoli, detached florets

DIRECTIONS:

1. Whisk together the stock, oyster sauce, soy sauce, garlic and sesame oil in a bowls until well incorporated. Add the slices of beef and toss to coat the beef evenly with the sauce.

2. Transfer the meat into the inner cooking pot and pour in the sauce. Place the inner cooking pot into the rice cooker, turn on and press the white rice button. Cook for 20 minutes while stirring occasionally or until the sauce starts to thicken and the meat is cooked through.

3.   Close the lid and switch to keep warm mode. Cook for 10 minutes more with low heat until the desired sauce consistency is achieved.

4.   If the sauce is not yet thick, whisk together the 2 tablespoons of water and corn starch in a cup and add into the beef. Reset the rice cooker, stir in the broccoli and cook until the sauce has thickened and the broccoli is tender.

5.   Transfer into a serving bowl or dish and serve immediately.

GARLIC SHRIMP

Preparation time: 5 minutes

Cooking time: 25 minutes

Yields: 4

INGREDIENTS:

2 to 3 teaspoons of cooking oil

1-inch fresh ginger root, minced

1 cup uncooked jasmine rice

1 teaspoon table salt, divided

1 cup of canned coconut milk, divided

4 tablespoons of water

1/4 cup loosely packed fresh cilantro leaves, chopped

2 pounds of fresh shrimps, peeled and deveined

3 garlic cloves, minced

4 to 5 teaspoons of sugar

2 tablespoons of cooking or olive oil

½ tablespoon of chili paste

2 teaspoons zest of lime

1 cup of trimmed fresh snap peas, blanched

DIRECTIONS:

1. Combine together the sugar, ¼ teaspoon salt, chili paste, garlic, olive oil in a large bowl and mix until well incorporated. Add the shrimp and toss to coat the shrimp evenly with the sauce.

2.   Place the inner cooking pot into the rice cooker, turn on and press the white rice button. Add in half of the shrimp into the inner pot and cook for 2 minutes on each side, or until the shrimp turns opaque. Turn the shrimp to cook the other side, remove from the inner pot and cook the remaining shrimp.

3.   When the shrimp are done, return the cooked shrimp into the inner pot and add 3 tablespoons of coconut milk and lime zest. Cook until it reaches to a boil, season to taste with salt and pepper and set aside.

4.   Return the inner cooking pot into the rice cooker, press the white rice button and add the oil. Once the oil is hot, sauté ginger for 1 minute and stir in ¼ teaspoon salt and the rice. Stir to combine and then pour in 1 cup of coconut milk and ¼ cup of stock. Close the lid and cook until the rice is fluffy and cooked through. When the rice cooker switches to keep warm mode, add the cilantro and fluff the rice with the serving spatula.

5.   Portion the rice into individual serving bowls and serve immediately with garlic shrimp on top.

Asian Main Course Recipes

SESAME GINGER CHICKEN

Preparation time: 10 minutes

Cooking time: 1 hour 45 minutes to 2 hours

Yields: 4

INGREDIENTS:

2 teaspoons sesame oil

4 chicken thighs, bone-in and skinned

Oil, for greasing

3 to 4 tablespoons light soy sauce

1 ½ to 2 tablespoons of brown sugar

½ fresh orange, juiced

1 ½ tablespoons of hoisin sauce

1-inch fresh ginger root, minced

2 garlic cloves, minced

Mixture of 2 teaspoons corn starch and 1 tablespoon

½ tablespoons of sesame seeds, toasted

2 medium stems of green onions, chopped

DIRECTIONS:

1. Place the inner cooking pot into the rice cooker, turn on and press the white rice button. Add the oil and brown for 4 minutes on each side. Turn to cook the other side and cook for 4 minutes.

2. Combine together the light soy sauce, orange juice, sugar, ginger and hoisin sauce in a bowl and mix until well incorporated. Pour the mixture in to the inner cooking pot and close the lid. Cook for

15 minutes while turning after the first 10 minutes to cook evenly on both sides. Switch to keep warm mode and cook for 1 hour or until the sauce has thickened. Remove the chicken and transfer into plate.

3. Add the water-cornstarch mixture in the inner pot, press the white rice button and cook until the sauce has thickened while stirring regularly.

4. Pour the sauce over the chicken and serve immediately with chopped green onions on top.

SWEET AND SOUR PORK

Preparation time: 10 minutes

Cooking time: 40 to 45 minutes

Yields: 4

INGREDIENTS:

1 pound spare ribs, cut into cubes

Marinade

1-inch fresh ginger root, sliced into juliennes

1 tablespoon white sugar

2 tablespoons brown sugar

2 to 3 teaspoons of oyster sauce

1 tablespoon sake or any rice wine

½ tablespoon light soy sauce

½ tablespoon soy sauce

½ cup of water

2 tablespoons cane vinegar

1 tablespoon tomato paste

1 stem of spring onions, chopped for serving

DIRECTIONS:

1. Place the bone into the inner cooking pot and add water to cover the meat. Turn on the rice cooker and press the white rice button. Close the lid and bring to a boil. Transfer into a bowl and let it stand for 10 minutes. Drain and set aside.

2. Combine together all ingredients for the marinade in a non-reactive container and mix it thoroughly until well incorporated. Pour the marinade into the bowl with meat and toss to coat the meat evenly. Cover and marinate in a chiller for 1 hour.

3. Turn on the rice cooker and press the white rice button, add the meat and brown on all sides or for about 5 minutes. Pour in the marinade, briefly stir and close the lid. Cook for about 30 minutes or until the sauce has thickened. Stir the ingredients after the first 15 minutes to avoid the sauce from burning.

4. When the meat is done, switch to keep warm mode and let it cook with low heat before serving.

5. Transfer into a serving dish or bowl and serve immediately with chopped spring onions on top.

THAI CHICKEN

Preparation time: 15 minutes

Cooking time: 30 to 35 minutes

Yields: 3 to 4

INGREDIENTS:

½ cup of light soy sauce

4 garlic cloves, minced

1-inch fresh ginger root, minced

1 tablespoon of hot chili sauce, or as needed for extra heat

1 pound chicken thighs, skin removed

1 medium green onion, chopped

2 to 3 teaspoons of toasted sesame oil

2 teaspoons of brown sugar

1 red onion, sliced into rounds

½ cup of water

2 to 3 tablespoons of peanut butter

DIRECTIONS:

1. Combine together the garlic, ginger, light soy sauce and hot chili sauce in a bowl and mix it thoroughly until well combined. Add the chicken and toss to coat the meat evenly with the sauce. Cover bowl and marinate for at least 1 hour.

2. Place the inner cooking pot into the rice cooker, turn on and press the white rice button. Add the oil and sauté the onions

until soft, stir in the chicken and marinade and cook for 5 minutes while stirring occasionally.

3.   Add ½ cup of boiling water, close lid and cook for 20 minutes, or until the chicken is tender and cooked through. Switch to keep warm mode and simmer for 10 more minutes. Stir in the peanut butter, briefly stir and transfer into a serving platter. Pour the sauce on top and serve immediately with chopped green onions on top.

SINGAPORE CHILI PRAWNS

Preparation time: 15 minutes

Cooking time: 20 minutes

Yields: 4

INGREDIENTS:

Sauce:

¾ cup of water

¼ cup of tomato catsup

2 to 3 tablespoons of brown sugar, as needed to taste

1 tablespoon of corn flour

½ tablespoon dark miso

1 pinch of salt

Prawns:

2 cups of fresh prawns, rinsed and drained, sliced across the back and deveined

2 tablespoons of cooking oil

6 garlic cloves, minced

6 red chili, chopped

1 medium whole egg

1 large scallions, cut into long 2-inch pieces

½ lime, juiced

¼ cup loosely packed fresh cilantro leaves, cut into chiffonades

DIRECTIONS:

1. Combine together all ingredients for the sauce in a bowl and mix it well until well combined. Set aside.

2. Place the inner cooking pot into the rice cooker, turn and press the white rice button. Add the oil and sauté the garlic and chili for 2 minutes or until lightly brown and aromatic. Add the prawns and cook for 3 minutes, or until opaque while turning to cook the other side. Pour in the sauce mixture and briefly stir to coat the shrimp.

3. Break the egg and slowly add into the inner pot, streak the egg with a fork to form long white streaks in the sauce. Close the lid and switch to keep warm mode. Cook for 10 minutes and stir in the lime juice and scallions. Close the lid and maintain keep warm mode before serving.

4. Transfer the prawns on a serving platter, pour the sauce on top and serve immediately.

KUNG PAO SHRIMP

Preparation time: 20 minutes

Cooking time: 20 to 25 minutes

Yields: 4

INGREDIENTS:

For the Shrimp

1 tablespoon of sake

1 tablespoon of cornstarch

½ teaspoon of salt

1 pound fresh shrimp, peeled and deveined

For the Sauce

2 teaspoons of sugar

3 tablespoons of water

2 to 3 teaspoons of balsamic vinegar

2 to 3 teaspoons of light soy sauce

½ tablespoon cornstarch

½ tablespoon of toasted sesame oil

Remaining Ingredients

1 tablespoon canola oil

½ cup green bell pepper, sliced into strips

2 teaspoons minced garlic

1-inch fresh ginger root, minced

3 dried hot red chili, crushed

2 tablespoons dry-roasted peanuts, chopped

2 cups of cooked rice

DIRECTIONS:

1. Combine together the sake wine, cornstarch and salt in a bowl until well combined. Add the shrimp and toss to coat evenly with the cornstarch mixture. Set aside.

2. In a separate bowl, combine together all ingredients for the sauce until well combined. Set aside.

3. Place the inner cooking pot into the rice cooker, turn on and press the white rice button. Add the oil and sauté the garlic, ginger, bell pepper and chili until lightly brown and aromatic. Stir in the shrimp mixture and cook for 5 minutes or until the shrimp turns opaque. Add the sauce, briefly stir and close the lid. Cook for 5 minutes or until the sauce has thickened. Switch to keep warm mode and cook for 15 minutes more, or until the sauce has thickened.

4. Portion rice into individual serving bowls or dishes and serve immediately with chopped peanuts on top.

Middle Eastern Main Course Recipes

SAUDI FISH CURRY

Preparation time: 15 minutes

Cooking time: 40 minutes

Yields: 4 to 6

INGREDIENTS:

1 pound white fish fillets, pat dried and cut into serving portions

table salt, to taste

2 tablespoons of clarified butter/ghee (butter or oil)

1 large onion, diced

1-inch piece of fresh ginger root, minced

1 teaspoon minced garlic

½ tablespoon chili powder

½ tablespoon Baharat spice mix (Baharat Aka Middle East Mixed Spices - the Real Mix)

½ tablespoon ground turmeric

1-inch piece of cinnamon bark

1 cup of canned diced tomatoes

1 loomi (dried lime), punctured with holes

½ cup of water

DIRECTIONS:

1. Season fish with salt and set aside.

2. Place the inner cooking pot into the rice cooker, turn on and press the white rice button. Add the ghee and sauté the onions, ginger, garlic, chili, Baharat spice, turmeric and cinnamon bark

and cook until lightly brown and aromatic. Stir in the loomi, tomatoes and water in the pot and season with salt. Close the lid and bring to a boil. Switch to keep warm mode and simmer for 15 minutes.

3.   Stir in the fish, close the lid immediately and cook for 20 minutes, or until the fish is thoroughly cooked.

4.   Remove the cinnamon and loomi and discard. Remove the fish with a slotted spoon and pour the sauce on top of the fish. Serve immediately.

CHICKEN TIKKA MASALA

Preparation time: 30 minutes

Cooking time: 3 hours

Yields: 4 to 6

INGREDIENTS:

For the spice mixture

3 tablespoons smoked paprika

3 tablespoons ground cumin

1 ½ ground coriander

1 ½ ground turmeric

½ tablespoon cayenne pepper

For the marinade

1 ½ pounds chicken thighs, skinned and cut into small pieces

¾ cup of plain yogurt

1 teaspoon minced garlic

1-inch piece fresh ginger root, minced

1 lemon, juiced

Other ingredients

1 red onion, diced

1 tablespoon minced garlic

1 cup of canned tomatoes

¾ cup of cream

½ cup loosely packed fresh cilantro leaves, roughly chopped

Oil or butter, for greasing

DIRECTIONS:

1. Combine all ingredients for the spice mix in a bowl and mix until well combined. Reserve half of the mixture while mix the other half with the chicken. Marinate the chicken for at least 1 hour. Pat dry chicken pieces with paper towels and set aside.

2. Mix half of the spice blend with the marinade ingredients and marinate chicken for 2 to 4 hours.

3. Place the inner cooking pot into the rice cooker, turn on and press the white rice button. Add and melt 2 tablespoons of butter and brown the chicken on all sides until the chicken is thoroughly cooked. Remove from the inner cooking pot and set aside.

4. Add ½ tablespoon in the inner cooking pot, sauté the onions and garlic until lightly brown and soft. Stir in the reserved spice mix and tomatoes, close the lid and cook for 15 minutes. Remove the mixture from the inner cooking pot, transfer to a bowl and let it cool. Transfer into a food processor and puree until smooth.

5. Return the pureed mixture into the inner cooking pot and the chicken, close the lid and bring to a boil. Switch to keep warm mode and cook for 20 minutes, or until the chicken is done. You can maintain keep warm mode for 4 hours.

6. Before serving, stir in the cream and cilantro, reset the rice cooker and bring to a boil.

7. Transfer the chicken and sauce into a serving dish and serve immediately.

CHICKEN TANGINE

Preparation time: 15 minutes

Cooking time: 1 hour 30 minutes to 2 hours

Yields: 4

INGREDIENTS:

1 teaspoon of extra virgin olive oil

1 pound of lamb meat, trimmed and cut into cubes

3 threads of saffron

1 red onion, diced

1 cup white long-grain rice, rinsed

2 cups Campbell's Real Stock Chicken

1 ½ cup beef stock

1 cup green olives, stuffed with semi-dried tomatoes

DIRECTIONS:

1. Place the inner cooking pot into the rice cooker, turn on and press the white rice button to start cooking. Add the oil and brown half of the lamb on all sides in the inner cooking pot, remove and brown the remaining lamb. Transfer into a plate and set aside.

2. Add the saffron and onions and cook until soft and aromatic. Stir in the rice and add the stock, close lid and bring to a boil. Cook for about 5 minutes, or until the rice is almost cooked through.

3. Add the lamb on top, close the lid and cook for 30 minutes or until the rice cooker switches to keep warm mode. When the lamb and rice is thoroughly cooked, remove the lamb and place

in a plate. Add the olives into the rice and fluff with the serving spatula.

4. Potion the rice into individual serving plates and serve with lamb meat on top.

BRAISED LAMB CHOPS

Preparation time: 15 minutes

Cooking time: 2 hours to 2 hours 30 minutes

Yields: 4

INGREDIENTS:

1 ½ tablespoons of extra virgin olive oil
4 lamb chops, chopped in to 2 portions
1 white onion, diced
½ cup of chicken stock
½ cup of white wine
¼ cup of dried tomatoes
½ tablespoon of dried thyme
¼ teaspoon of cumin powder
1 cup canned white beans, drained
Salt and crushed black pepper, to taste
2 cups of cooked rice, for serving

DIRECTIONS:

1. Place the inner cooking pot into the rice cooker, turn on and press the white rice button to start cooking. Brown the lamb chops on both sides or for about 20 minutes. Add the onions into the inner cooking pot and cook until soft, stir in the thyme, tomatoes, cumin, white wine and the stock. Close the lid securely and bring to a boil. Cook for about an hour and switch to keep warm mode. Cook for 1 more hour with low heat or until the lamb is cooked through.

2. Stir in the beans and reset the rice cooker, cook for 30 minutes or until the lamb is very tender and the beans is cooked through. Season to taste with salt and pepper and switch to keep warm mode.

3. Portion the rice into individual serving bowls and serve warm with lamb and sauce on top.

STUFFED CABBAGE ROLLS

Preparation time: 30 minutes

Cooking time: 3 minutes

Yields: 4

INGREDIENTS:

8 leaves cabbage

¾ cup of cooked white rice

1 medium whole egg, beaten

4 tablespoons of milk

1 small onion, minced

¾ pounds of ground lean beef

1 teaspoon of salt

1 teaspoon of crushed black pepper

1 cup of canned tomato sauce

2 teaspoons of brown sugar

2 teaspoons of lemon juice

½ tablespoon of Worcestershire sauce

DIRECTIONS:

1. Add water in the inner cooking pot and place into the rice cooker. Turn on the rice cooker, bring to a boil and blanch the cabbage leaves for 2 minutes. Remove from the inner cooking pot and drain.

2. Combine together the cooked rice, milk, onion, egg, beef and season to taste with salt and pepper. Mix the ingredients thoroughly until well combined.

3. Add 2 tablespoons of the meat mixture on the center of the cabbage leaf. Fold over the bottom side to cover the stuffing, fold both sides and roll it upwards. Repeat the procedure with the remaining ingredients.

4. Place the cabbage rolls into the inner cooking pot. You may need to arrange them in two layers if needed.

5. Combine together the sugar, lemon juice, tomato juice and Worcestershire sauce in a mixing bowl and pour into the inner pot with the cabbage rolls.

6. Close the lid and cook until it reaches to a boil. Switch to keep warm mode and cook for 3 to 4 hours or until the rice and meat is cooked through.

7. Before serving, reset the rice cooker and return it to a boil. Season to taste with salt and pepper.

8. Carefully transfer the cabbage rolls into as serving dish and serve warm with sauce on top.

European
Main Course Recipes

MEDITERRANEAN CHICKEN RICE

Preparation time: 5 minutes

Cooking time: 20 minutes

Yields: 4 to 6

INGREDIENTS:

1 ½ tablespoons of cooking oil

1 white onion, diced

1 crushed garlic clove

1 cup cooked shredded chicken mat

2 cups of short-grain rice, rinsed

2 teaspoons poultry seasoning

2 tablespoons of lemon zest

¼ cup of loosely packed fresh parsley leaves, minced

Crushed black pepper, to taste

boiling water

DIRECTIONS:

1. Place the inner cooking pot into the rice cooker, turn on and press the white rice button. Add the oil and sauté the onion and garlic until soft and translucent. Stir in the rice and chicken and sauté for 2 minutes. Pour in with boiling water to fill up to line 2. Add the poultry seasoning and stir to combine, close the lid and cook until the rice is tender or until it switches to keep warm mode. Season with crushed pepper, stir and cook for 5 more minutes.

2.   Pour the contents from the inner cooking pot into a strainer to separate the rice and chicken. Return the rice and chicken into the inner cooking pot, add the lemon zest and parsley and toss to combine.

3.   Portion into individual serving dishes and serve immediately.

ITALIAN MEATBALLS

Preparation time: 10 minutes

Cooking time: 30 to 40 minutes

Yields: 4 to 6

INGREDIENTS:

1 cup of ready-made marinara sauce

3 cups of water

½ pound of linguini pasta

1 pound of frozen meatballs

2 teaspoons of minced garlic

¼ cup of loosely packed fresh parsley leaves, minced

1 teaspoon of Italian mixed herbs

¼ cup Parmesan cheese, grated

DIRECTIONS:

1. Place the inner cooking pot into the rice cooker and add all ingredients except for the pasta and meatballs. Turn in the rice cooker and press the white rice button. Stir to combine the ingredients, close the lid and bring to a boil.

2. Add the pasta and meatballs and cook for about 20 minutes. Or until the pasta is cooked to al dente and the meatballs is cooked through.

3. If the sauce is yet thick and the pasta is not yet done, reset the rice cooker and cook until the desired thickness is achieved or until the pasta is done.

4. and cook for 20 minutes. Test pasta for doneness. Place the lid back on the .cooker. If necessary, cook several minutes longer until pasta is tender.

5. Portion into individual serving dishes and serve immediately with grated Parmesan cheese on top.

Spicy Lemon Spanish Chicken

Preparation time: 20 minutes

Cooking time: 4 hours

Yields: 4

INGREDIENTS:

2 tablespoons of flour

1 ½ tablespoons of smoked paprika

2 to 3 teaspoons of garlic powder

Salt and coarsely ground pepper, to taste

4 to 6 chicken thighs

3 to 4 tablespoons of canola oil

1 cup of canned stewed tomatoes

1 large bell pepper, seeded and diced

1 white onion, sliced into rounds

3 tablespoons of tomato paste

2 cups of low sodium chicken stock

1 cup of long-grain rice, rinsed and drained

1 teaspoon of dried red pepper, crushed

1 organic lemon, juiced and zested

½ cup pimiento stuffed green olives

DIRECTIONS:

1. Combine together the flour, salt, pepper, garlic powder, paprika in a bowl and add the meat. Toss to coat the chicken and transfer into a resealable plastic bag. Set aside.

2. Place the inner cooking pot into the rice cooker, turn on and press the white rice button to start cooking. Add the oil and heat the oil until smoking, add the chicken and brown for on all sides for about 5 minutes on each side. Turn to brown the other side and transfer into a plate.

3. Add the tomatoes, onions and bell peppers into the inner cooking pot. Return the chicken into the pot and place it over the vegetables, pour in the tomato paste and the stock and close the lid. Cook for 1 hour or until the chicken is cooked through, briefly stir and switch to keep warm mode. Simmer for another 1 hour or until the sauce has reduced and thickened.

4. Remove the chicken mixture, transfer into a large bowl and cover to keep it warm. Add the rice, pepper flakes, juice and zest of lemon. Pour with water to fill up to line 2 and season to taste with salt and pepper. Press the white rice button and cook until the rice is tender and cooked through, or until it switches to keep warm mode. Fluff the rice with the serving spatula and portion into individual serving dish.

5. Top each dish with chicken and vegetables, drizzle with extra lemon juice on top and serve immediately.

BEEF BURGUNDY

Preparation time: 17 minutes

Cooking time: 20 minutes

Yields: 4 to 6

INGREDIENTS:

1 pound beef chuck roast, bone removed and cut into 1-inch cubes

2 large carrots, peeled and diced

2 cups of canned mushrooms, quartered or halved

½ cup of onion wedges

1 teaspoon of minced garlic

1 bay leaf

½ teaspoon salt and ½ teaspoon of black pepper, to taste

½ to 1 teaspoon of dried thyme leaves

¾ to 1 cup of beef stock

¾ cup red wine

3 tablespoons of tomato paste

1 ½ tablespoons of flour

3 to 4 tablespoons of water

2 cups cooked egg noodles

DIRECTIONS:

1. Place the beef, carrots, onions, mushrooms, bay leaf, garlic, thyme, black pepper, salt, stock, wine and the tomato paste into the inner cooking pot. Place the inner cooking pot into the rice

cooker, turn and press the white rice button. Close the lid and cook for about 1 hour and 30 minutes, or until the beef is almost tender.

2. While cooking the beef, combine together the flour and water in a bowl and mix until the flour is completely dissolved. Pour the mixture into the inner cooking pot and briefly stir to combine. Switch to keep warm mode and cook until thick and the beef is thoroughly cooked.

3. Portion the cooked noodles into individual serving dish or bowls and serve immediately with beef stew on top.

RATATOUILLE

Preparation time: 20 minutes

Cooking time: 1 hour 30 minutes

Yields: 4

INGREDIENTS:

1 cup of diced carrots

1 cup diced potatoes

1 cup chopped zucchinis

1/2 white onion

2 red tomatoes, seeded and diced

1 teaspoon minced garlic

1 ½ tablespoons of cooking oil

½ tablespoon of dried basil

Crushed black pepper, to taste

Table salt, to taste

1 cup of vegetable stock

1 tablespoon minced fresh rosemary leaves

1 tablespoon minced fresh thyme leaves

DIRECTIONS:

1. Place the inner cooking pot into the rice cooker, turn on and press the white rice button. Add the oil and sauté the onions, garlic and tomatoes until soft and tender. Stir in the diced vegetables, dried herbs and season to taste with salt and pepper.

Stir to combine and pour in the stock. Close the lid and cook for 1 hour or until the vegetables are tender and cooked through.

2. Switch to keep warm mode, briefly stir and cook for another 5 minutes. Transfer into a serving dish and serve immediately.

American
Main Course Recipes

SHRIMP JAMBALAYA

Preparation time: 15 minutes

Cooking time: 30 minutes

Yields: 4 to 6

INGREDIENTS:

1 cup canned button mushroom, halved

2 garlic clove, finely minced

1 link of sweet Italian sausage, casing removed and chopped

1 small red onion, finely diced

1 small bell pepper, diced

2 ½ cups of chicken stock

2 cups of cooked shrimp, peeled and deveined

1 tablespoon of clarified butter

1 ½ cups of long-grain white rice

1 cup canned diced tomatoes

1 teaspoon of cayenne pepper

DIRECTIONS:

1. Place the inner cooking pot into the rice cooker, turn on and press the white rice button. Add the sausage and cook until brown while stirring occasionally. Drain the excess fat and add the clarified butter, stir in the garlic, onions, bell pepper and mushrooms and cook for 5 minutes, until the onions are soft and the vegetables are tender.

2. Stir in the remaining ingredients, briefly stir to combine and close the lid. Bring it to a boil and cook for about 15 to 20

minutes, or until the rice is cooked through. When the rice is done and the rice cooker has switched to keep warm mode, fluff the rice with the serving spatula.

3. Maintain keep warm mode for 10 minutes and portion into individual serving bowls. Serve warm with extra cayenne pepper for added heat.

PHILLY CHEESESTEAKS

Preparation time: 20 minutes

Cooking time: 2 to 3 hours

Yields: 4

INGREDIENTS:

1 large onion, halved crosswise and thinly sliced

1 large bell peppers, halved lengthwise and thinly sliced

2 cups of beef top sirloin steak, thinly sliced into strips

1 package of onion soup mix

2 cups of beef stock

4 hoagie buns, sliced in the middle

8 slices of provolone cheese

Pickled spice cherry peppers, chopped

DIRECTIONS:

1. Place the inner cooking pot into the rice cooker, add the onion, bell pepper, beef, onion soup mix and pour in the stock. Stir to combine, close the lid and cook for about 1 hour or until the rice cooker switches to keep warm mode.

2. Maintain keep warm mode for 1 hour and reset the rice cooker to cook for another cooking interval. When the beef is very tender, prepare the buns and other ingredients.

3. Split the buns and add the cheese on one side, top with beef slices and add a layer of cherry peppers. Serve immediately.

SLOPPY JOES

Preparation time: 20 minutes

Cooking time: 3 hours

Yields: 6

INGREDIENTS:

1 pound of lean beef, ground

1 medium stalk of celery, diced

1 medium onion, diced

1 cup chili sauce, for serving

1 ½ tablespoons of sugar

2 teaspoons sweet pickle relish

2 teaspoon of Worcestershire sauce

½ teaspoon table salt

¼ teaspoon of crushed black pepper

6 burger buns, split

DIRECTIONS:

1. Place the inner cooking pot into the rice cooker and add the ground beef, celery and onions. Turn on the rice cooker and press the white rice button, close the lid and cook until the meat is no longer pink while stirring occasionally.

2. Drain excess fat and stir in the sugar, chili sauce, pickle relish, Worcestershire sauce and season with salt and pepper. Close the lid and cook for 1 hour or until the rice cooker switches to keep warm mode. Maintain keep warm mode for 30 minutes and remove the inner cooking pot from the rice cooker.

3. Add ½ cup of meat mixture on top of each bun and serve.

PULLED PORK

Preparation time: 5 minutes

Cooking time: 2 hours

Yields: 6

INGREDIENTS:

1 ½ pound of pork loin, excess fat trimmed

1 ½ cups stock or broth

1 ½ cups of water

1 cup of any barbecue sauce

1 teaspoon crushed black pepper

1 teaspoon of salt

DIRECTIONS:

1. Add all ingredients except for the meat in the inner cooking pot, stir to combine and place the inner cooking pot into the rice cooker. Add the meat, turn on the rice cooker and press the white rice button. Close the lid and cook for about 2 hours or until the meat is fork tender.

2. If the rice cooker switched to keep warm mode and not yet done, reset and cook until the meat is tender. After the rice cooker has switched to keep warm mode for the second time, it is done.

3. Transfer the meat into a large bowl, let it cool and shred it with two forks.

4. Serve the shredded meat with choice of bun or bread.

SWEET 'N' TANGY CHICKEN WINGS

Preparation time: 20 minutes

Cooking time: 2 hours

Yields: 6 to 8

INGREDIENTS:

1 pound Wingettes of chicken

½ teaspoon of salt, divided

½ teaspoon crushed pepper

1 cup of preferred ketchup

4 tablespoon of brown sugar

4 tablespoons of red wine vinegar

1 tablespoon of Worcestershire sauce

2 teaspoon of Dijon mustard

1 garlic clove, minced

1 teaspoon of toasted sesame seeds, optional

DIRECTIONS:

1. Season the chicken with salt and crushed peppers and add into the inner cooking pot. Place the inner cooking pot into the rice cooker, turn on and press the white rice button. Brown the chicken on all sides and stir in the remaining ingredients.

2. Stir the ingredients until well combined, close the lid and cook for 1 hour or until the chicken is cooked through. Stir the ingredients well and cook until the sauce has thickened or according to preferred thickness.

3. Sprinkle with toasted sesame seeds and toss to combine. Switch to keep warm mode and let it cook with low heat before serving.

4. Transfer into individual serving dish and serve immediately.

10

DESSERT

Rice Cooker
Dessert Recipes

RICE PUDDING, INDIAN STYLE

Preparation time: 5 minutes

Cooking time: 1 hour to 1 hour 30 minutes

Yields: 3 to 4

INGREDIENTS:

½ cup of Basmati rice or any long-grain rice, rinsed and drained

3 cup of milk, or as needed

½ cup packed sugar, or as needed according to taste

2 tablespoons slivered almonds

1 cardamom pod

DIRECTIONS:

1. Place all ingredients into the inner cooking pot and stir to combine. Transfer the inner cooking pot into the rice cooker, turn on and press the white rice button to start cooking. Close the lid and cook for about 1 hour or until it switches to keep warm mode. Open the lid after the first 30 minutes of cooking to avoid over spilling of the inner pot contents and check regularly.

2. When the mixture has thickened and the rice has softened already, switch to keep warm mode and let it stand for 10 minutes. You can add more milk and adjust the taste by adding more milk and sugar until the desired consistency and taste is achieved.

3. Remove the inner cooking pot and portion the rice pudding into serving bowls. Serve warm with almonds on top.

TATIN CAKE

Preparation time: 15 minutes

Cooking time: 1 hour to 1 hour 30 minutes

Yields: 3 to 4

INGREDIENTS:

2 apples, cored and sliced into wedges

2 tablespoons butter

3 tablespoons brown sugar

½ cup flour, sifted

¼ cup white sugar

½ teaspoon of baking powder

Pinch of salt

3 tablespoons of butter, melted

2 medium whole eggs

DIRECTIONS:

1. Combine together the flour, white sugar, baking powder and salt in a mixing bowl and mix in 3 tablespoons of melted butter and the eggs. Mix it thoroughly until well combined and set aside.

2. Place the inner cooking pot into the rice cooker and the butter. Transfer the inner cooking pot into the rice cooker, turn the rice cooker on and press the white rice button to melt the butter.

3. Once the butter has melted, add the apples and cook for 5 minutes while tossing frequently to cook them evenly. Stir in the brown sugar and cook until the sugar starts to caramelise.

4. Arrange the apple wedges on the bottom of the pan and add in the batter mixture on top. With a serving spatula, even out the dough and cover the apples completely.

5. Close the lid and cook for about 20 to 25 minutes or until done. It is done when a toothpick inserted on the thickest part comes out clean. Switch to keep warm mode and let it stand for 10 minutes.

6. Carefully flip the inner cooking pot upside down onto a serving dish and serve immediately.

BANANA PUDDING WITH CARAMEL SAUCE

Preparation time: 15 minutes

Cooking time: 45 to 50 minutes

Yields: 4

INGREDIENTS:

Banana Pudding

2 tablespoons of melted butter

4 tablespoons unsalted melted butter

2 tablespoons packed brown sugar

3 tablespoons brown sugar

1 ripe banana, peeled sliced into rounds

2 ripe bananas, peeled and mashed

1 medium whole egg, beaten

2 small pinches or ½ teaspoon of cinnamon spice powder

2 to 3 tablespoons of milk

1 cup of sifted self-rising flour

Caramel sauce, for serving

DIRECTIONS:

1. Combine together 4 tablespoons of melted butter, egg, 3 tablespoons of sugar, cinnamon, mashed banana and milk in a large mixing bowl. Mix it thoroughly until well combined. Mix in the flour into the banana mixture and mix again until well incorporated. Set aside.

2. Lightly grease the inner cooking pot with oil and line with parchment paper. Pour in 2 tablespoons of melted butter and sprinkle 2 tablespoons of sugar evenly on the inner pot. Place a layer of the sliced ripe bananas over the butter and sugar mixture.

3. Add the flour and mashed banana mixture into the inner cooking pot and spread with the serving spatula evenly.

4. Turn on the rice cooker and press the white rice button. Close the lid and cook for about 20 to 25 minutes or until the top part is done. It is done when a toothpick inserted on the thickest part comes out clean. When it is done, switch to keep warm mode and let it stand for 10 minutes before serving.

5. Carefully flip the inner cooking pot upside down onto a serving plate and serve immediately with caramel sauce on top.

CHOCOLATE STEEL CUT OATS

Preparation time: 5 minutes

Cooking time: 1 hour to 1 hour 30 minutes

Yields: 4

INGREDIENTS:

1 cup steel cut oats

2 cups water

1 cup of milk

1 tablespoon cocoa powder

2 tablespoons of sugar, or as needed according to taste

2 tablespoons of chocolate chips, for serving

DIRECTIONS:

1. Place the inner cooking pot into the rice cooker and add all ingredients except for the chocolate chips. Stir the ingredients, turn on the rice cooker and press the white rice button to start cooking. Close the lid and cook for about 1 hour or until the oats are soft and the consistency has thickened.

2. Switch to keep warm mode and let it stand for 10 minutes. You can also add more milk and sugar according to preferred consistency or taste is achieved.

3. Portion cooked chocolate oats into individual serving bowls and serve warm with chocolate chips on top.

POACHED PEARS IN POMEGRANATE

Preparation time: 5 minutes

Cooking time: 50 minutes

Yields: 4

INGREDIENTS:

2 firm ripe and slim pears, core and peeled, cut into half

1 ½ to 2 cups of pomegranate juice

1 cup apple cider

1 cup apple juice

3-inch stick of cinnamon

1 clove

1 star anise

1 cardamom pod

1-inch piece of fresh ginger root, grated

DIRECTIONS:

1. Place the inner cooking pot into the rice cooker and add in the juices, apple cider, cinnamon, star anise, clove, cardamom and ginger. Stir the ingredients well and add the pear halves into the inner cooking pot. Close the lid, turn on the rice cooker and press the white rice button. Cook pears for about 50 minutes, or until the pears are tender.

2. Switch to keep warm mode and turn the pears over to cook and coat the other side with the poaching liquid. Close the lid and let it stand for an hour.

3.   Remove the pears carefully from the inner cooking pot and serve warm or chilled.

CHOCOLATE LAVA CAKE

Preparation time: 15 minutes

Cooking time: 1 hour to 1 hour 30 minutes

Yields: 4 to 6

INGREDIENTS:

1 package or box of chocolate moist cake mix

Other needed ingredients for the cake mix

1 can (16 oz) of Betty Crocker milk chocolate frosting, divided

Oil, for greasing

DIRECTIONS:

1. Place the half of the chocolate frosting mixture in small bowl and chill 1 before cooking.

2. Combine together all ingredients for the chocolate cake in a mixing bowl and mix until well incorporated.

3. Lightly grease the inner cooking pot with oil and place into the rice cooker. Pour in half of the cake batter and add the chilled chocolate frosting on the center. Pour in the remaining cake batter and close the lid securely. Turn on the rice cooker and press the white rice button to start cooking.

4. Cook for 25 to 30 minutes or until the batter on the top part is almost done. Close the lid and switch to keep warm mode. Cook for another 30 minutes until the cake is done.

5. It is done when a toothpick inserted on the part where there is no chocolate frosting comes out clean.

6. When the cake is done, gently flip the inner cooking pot upside down onto a serving plate. Set aside and let it rest.

7. Return the inner cooking pot into the rice cooker and press the white rice button. Pour in the reserved chocolate frosting and cook until warmed through.

8. Pour the chocolate frosting over the cake and serve immediately.

ALMOND CREAM COCONUT FLAN

Preparation time: 10 minutes

Cooking time: 50 minutes

Yields: 6

INGREDIENTS:

2 cups of water, for steaming

4 egg yolks

¼ cup of sugar

A pinch of salt

2 cups of heavy cream

½ tablespoon of almond extract

½ cup of shredded coconut

DIRECTIONS:

1. Place the inner cooking pot into the rice cooker and add the cream, half the sugar, shredded coconut and almond extract. Transfer the inner cooking pot into the rice cooker, turn on and press the white rice button. Cook the mixture for 5 minutes or until it starts to form bubbles while stirring regularly. Transfer into a bowl and let it rest to cool.

2. Return the inner cooking pot into the rice cooker, pour in 2 cups of water and press the power button. Close the lid, press the white rice or steam button and bring the water to a boil.

3. Whisk together half the cream, yolks, salt and half of the sugar in a mixing bowl until well combined.

4. Gradually add in the remaining cream while whisking constantly until well incorporated. Pour it into a baking dish with a size that fits into the inner cooking pot and steam tray. Cover the baking dish with aluminum foil and crimp the edges to seal. Place the baking dish on the steam tray.

5. Carefully open the lid of the rice cooker place the steam tray with the baking dish on the inner cooking pot. Close the lid and cook for about 50 minutes.

6. When the almond coconut cream is done, carefully remove the steam tray with a mitt and let the coconut flan rest for 10 minutes without the foil.

7. Serve almond coconut cream flan chilled or immediately after resting.

COCONUT BLACK RICE PUDDING

Preparation time: 5 minutes

Cooking time: 45 to 60 minutes

Yields: 3 to 4

INGREDIENTS:

1 cup of black glutinous rice, soaked for 2 hours and drained

3 cups of water

½ cup of brown sugar

1 cup canned coconut cream, for serving

DIRECTIONS:

1. Place the rice and water in the inner cooking pot, turn the rice cooker on and press the white rice button to start cooking. Close the lid and cook for about 1 hour until the rice is soft and tender and the consistency is thick. You may add more water and sugar to adjust taste and consistency if desired. Reset the rice cooker and manually switch to keep warm mode when done.

2. Add the sugar and switch to keep warm mode, stir and let it stand for 10 minutes until or until the sugar is completely dissolved.

3. Portion black rice pudding into individual serving bowls and drizzle with coconut cream on top. Serve warm.

CREAMY COCONUT FRUIT AND ROOT VEGGIES

Preparation time: 20 minutes

Cooking time: 45 to 50 minutes

Yields: 6 to 8

INGREDIENTS:

½ cup of diced sweet potatoes

½ cup of diced purple yam

½ cup of diced plantains

½ cup of ripe jackfruit, sliced into long strips

½ cup of cooked small tapioca pearls

½ cup of granulated sugar, or as needed

1 cup coconut milk

1 cup water

DIRECTIONS:

1.   Pour in the water and add the potatoes, yam, plantains and jackfruit in the inner cooking pot. Transfer the inner cooking into the rice cooker, turn in and press the white rice button. Close the lid and cook until the vegetables are almost tender, or for 30 minutes.

2.   Stir in the coconut milk, sugar and the tapioca in the inner cooking pot and close the lid. Cook for another 20 minutes or until the ingredients are cooked through and tender and the consistency has thickened.

3.   Switch to keep warm mode, adjust taste and consistency and let it stand for 10 minutes.

4.   Portion dessert soup into individual serving bowls and serve warm or cool.

CHAMPORADO (COCOA RICE PUDDING)

Preparation time: 5 minutes

Cooking time: 40 minutes

Yields: 4

INGREDIENTS:

½ cup of Arborio rice, rinsed and drained

2 cups of canned coconut milk

1 cup of water

¼ cup of unsweetened cocoa powder

½ cup raw cane or brown sugar

Evaporated milk, for serving

DIRECTIONS:

1. Place the rice and water in to the inner cooking pot, turn on the rice cooker and press the white rice button. Close the lid and bring to a boil.

2. Add in the coconut milk, cocoa powder and sugar and close the lid. Cook for about 30 minutes or until the rice is soft and the consistency has thickened. Switch to keep warm mode and cook for 10 minutes more.

3. Portion Champurrado into individual serving bowls and drizzle with milk on top. Serve warm or cool.